THE
TROUT
BOHEMIA

Fly-fishing travels in New Zealand

DEREK
GRZELEWSKI

STACKPOLE
BOOKS

Text & photographs © Derek Grzelewski, 2013
Typographical design © David Bateman Ltd, 2013

Published in the United States by
STACKPOLE BOOKS
5067 Ritter Road
Mechanicsburg, PA 17055
www.stackpolebooks.com

ISBN 978-0-8117-1269-9

Published in 2013 by David Bateman Ltd
30 Tarndale Grove, Albany, Auckland, New Zealand
www.batemanpublishing.co.nz

Book design & maps: Nick Turzynski, redinc., Auckland
Cover artwork & illustrations: Stella Senior — www.evesart.co.nz

QUOTATION SOURCES:
Pages 9, 19 & 161 John Gierach, sourced online at http://en.wikipedia.org/wiki/
John_Gierach; p 53 Tom McGuane, *The Longest Silence* (Knopf, New York, 1999); pp 64,
65 & 66–67 Peggy Hamilton, *Wild Irishman: The Story of Bill Hamilton* (A.H. & A.W. Reed,
Wellington, 1969); p 68 Les Bloxham & Anne Stark, *Jet Boat: The Making of a New Zealand
Legend*, Reed Publishing, Auckland, 1994; p 71 Charles Gaines, *The Next Valley Over: An
Angler's Progress* (Crown Publishing Group, New York, 2000); p 83 Arnold Gingrich,
sourced online; p 96 Rick Bass, Winter, *Notes from Montana* (Mariner Books, Boston,
1991); pp 99 & 192 Edward Abbey, *Desert Solitaire: A Season in the Wilderness* (Ballantine Books,
New York, 1985); p 117 Norman Maclean, *A River Runs Through It* (University of Chicago
Press, Chicago, 1989); p 122 Barry Brailsford, *The Song of Waitaha: The Histories of a Nation*
(Ngatapuwae Trust, Christchurch, 1994); p 129, 134 & 137 Peter McIntyre, *Kakahi, New
Zealand* (Reed Publishing, Auckland, 1972); p 153 Janna Bialek, 'Thoughts from a Fishing
Past' in *Uncommon Waters* (Holly Morris ed., Seal Press, Seattle, 1998); p 181 Will Rogers,
sourced online at http://en.wikipedia.org/wiki/Will_Rogers

Printed in China through Colorcraft Ltd, Hong Kong

Contents

For my father Bogdan,
from the Happy Isles

'Once upon the time a prince met a beautiful princess.

  "Will you marry me?" the prince asked.

  The princess said, "No."

  And the prince lived happily ever after. And he fished, and skied, and hunted, and went on long safaris, and he drank expensive whiskies by the campfire, and there was no one there to tell him he played too much, and that it was costing a fortune . . .'

ANONYMOUS

'For us, New Zealand is a dream come true, the trout Bohemia.'

JETSKE DARBEAUD

'A seeker of silences am I.'

KHALIL GIBRAN, THE PROPHET

Prologue

'Is that it then? Is this how it all ends?' she asked, and I did not have the courage to meet her eyes.

For the past half an hour, with a heavy heart, I'd been telling Ella how this togetherness of ours was not working for me any more. How, after the autobahn of a long honeymoon, our road was getting more and more rocky and potholed, and how I was increasingly unsure I wanted to travel it. I'd been telling her how I grew tired of conflicts and dramas, how it seemed I was forever putting out fires and whenever one was out, another would flare up elsewhere until, in the end, I'd given up and thought, 'Well, just let them burn'.

All the time I talked, she held me with a steady gaze and listened silently, two rivulets of tears running down her beautiful sun-browned face. Now that at last she had spoken, asking the question loaded with so much finality, I could not bring myself to answer it.

Truth was I didn't know. Despite our best intentions and contrary to earlier promises and reassurances, we had lost our way. Maybe we just went into it all too hard and fast, two stubborn individuals burning with many passions but unable or unwilling to compromise. Or perhaps we were just not compatible. I really didn't know any more.

I could feel Ella's eyes probing me for answers, but the words failed me. I got up and gave her a peck on the cheek, tasting the saltiness of tears, then headed for the door. With my hand on the doorknob I turned to her one last time. She was still there on the couch, paralysed in stillness, her usually tall and proud ballerina's body crumpled as if the bones were suddenly gone from it and there was nothing to hold it up any more.

'I need to go away for a while,' I said. 'Let's put some time and space into this. Maybe then we can piece it all back together.'

For a couple of beats I waited for a word from her but, as none came, I stepped out through the door and slid it shut behind me. The metal frame gliding on rollers sounded like the fall of a guillotine. Whoosh! Maybe it was how it all ended.

THE TROUT BOHEMIA

chapter 1

'The solution to any problem — work, love,
money, whatever — is to go fishing, and the
worse the problem, the longer the trip should be.'

JOHN GIERACH

It was early October, in New Zealand the beginning of trout season. My 4WD camper was parked in the driveway, ready to go, and Maya, my Airedale terrier, was sitting in the driver's seat, waiting. As I was getting in, she gave me a double lick of greeting while her tail walloped the seat cover, raising puffs of sand. Then she moved over to the passenger side. It was her seat again, now that there were only two of us in the camper. I backed out on to the road and, once on the main highway, felt the Land Cruiser pick up its momentum.

I took a deep breath and it came out as a seismic sigh, and Maya's tail walloped three times like the clap of applause. It was time to cheer up, she was implying. As so many times in the past, and they were always good times, we were again 'Gone Fishing' together. Might be some time and out of range. Incommunicado. Address unknown. We were going to the best place we knew: to the peace, solitude and the silences of the rivers.

Two hours later we were in Southland, heading further into the vast green plains through which so many good trout rivers meander. In spring, Southland can be a volatile place and this time it was no different. Apocalyptic hail storms bore down on us like giant waves from the Roaring Forties, pelting the camper canopy with hailstones the size of peas. The ice bounced off the road and crunched under the tyres. There were bands of brilliant sunshine in-between the storms, and full, double-arch rainbows, and this stark illumination made the farm hills glow with surreal green, so bright it seemed almost fluorescent. It was blinding like the surface of a glacier but lush and fresh and dotted with the confetti of shorn sheep and lambs prancing on newly found legs.

The forecast was good so I was not too concerned about the passing tempests. Here and there along the way, at Anglers' Access signs and by numerous bridges, I saw fly-fishers' cars parked, each staking a claim of privacy to an upstream beat, but the opening-day fever was tapering off and I was confident that, like every early season over the past decade, I'd have 'my' river largely to myself.

By now, the sense that by driving away I was stretching some invisible rubber cord which would either snap or pull me back to Ella was gone, replaced by the gravitational pull of the river which was growing stronger. I hadn't been back here for nearly a year and the anticipation was delicious. Butterflies in the stomach. It felt like going to visit an old friend — solid and reliable, always welcoming and always there in times of need.

The river is not especially well known, nor is it a better fishery than any other waterway in Southland. But because of my experiences there — the rapid evolution of skills it had forced me into, the friendships and camaraderie I'd found there, the moments of magic so numerous and stacked so close together they overshadowed all other memories — it has always been a special place for me. Secret and sacred. The river of the heart.

Two years had passed since I completed *The Trout Diaries* and much had happened in the meantime. Firstly, like a doting teenager again, I had fallen in love just as when, this late in mid-life, I thought I was immune to such afflictions. Then there was the sad news from Grandpa Trout.

At the age of eighty-two, the itinerant Frenchman and my self-appointed fly-fishing mentor, decided he would not be coming to New Zealand any more. Although my river of the heart was also one of his most treasured places in the world, he reasoned that he had evaded old age and its associated infirmities long enough, and now they were catching up with him — strict diet, exercise regimen and happy river life notwithstanding. Nothing was wrong as such, but he had grown apprehensive about spending six months, much of it alone, in the backwoods of a country where he did not even speak the language.

He would still go to Quebec and the rivers of the Gaspé Peninsula for the Atlantic salmon season there, but it was unlikely we'd see him in New Zealand again, and for all those who had got to know him it was much sadder news than we dared to admit.

Grandpa bought a little apartment in France, not far from where he grew up, and he was back on his home river again, one where he learnt to fish as a boy. Some decades ago, the river's entire ecosystem had been wiped out by a toxic spill from a paper mill in its upper reaches, but the waterway was almost fully recovered, and large sea-run trout had entered it again, and they were cunning, intelligent fish, Grandpa assured me, adept at taunting the best of fishermen. They were impossible to catch, by the rest of us mere mortals anyway. In him, however, they might have just found their match. Perhaps all the fly-fishing he's done so far — the past twenty years of averaging some 300 river-days a year — was only training for this highest of challenges.

The last time I saw him was the season past in Reefton, in the campground where he always rented a cabin. The inside was suitably Spartan, just as he liked it, and he had his cooking gear set out. He made us *pommes frites* for dinner, French fries *comme il faut*, the way itinerant *fritiers* of old used to make them, hawking their fares from a cart towed by a bicycle. They deep-fried the potatoes twice — slow and at low heat first to cook them right through, then cranking up the temperature to expel the oil from the chips, and to leave them crisp on the outside but light and soft like a sponge under the crust.

Over those, a bifteck and a bottle of red, which he drank religiously now only because his French doctor had prescribed it, we got lost in our usual river talk. About the virtues of some leaders and tippets over others. Flies that worked well that season and the sure-fire ones that disappointed, about the fish that we remembered because of how we caught them and others, even more memorable, because they would not be fooled. And never once did he mention that we were seeing each other for the last time. I bade him a bon voyage and said I was looking forward to fishing with him again next season, and he just smiled and stood there by the doors of his cabin as I drove away.

Since the year of the *Diaries* I hadn't seen Henry Spencer either. I hadn't heard from him and, considering the fragile state he was in back then, I feared the worst. Maybe his battle with cancer was not such a clean win after all, not as clean as he wanted me to believe, wanted himself to believe perhaps. I could not imagine him in relapse, bed-ridden, hooked up to chemo and IV fluids. It would have been like putting a wild trout in an aquarium, with an oxygenating pump and a timer feeder. Too cruel to contemplate.

Yet while all this and more went on, the trout rivers continued to flow, ever fresh and self-renewing. To me, they are the epitome of change, a reminder that everything everywhere is in a state of flux, and that holding on, whether to memories or a pleasing status quo, is a futile effort. Because life is like a river, forever on the move.

I've made new river friends since the *Diaries*, although perhaps making friends is not the right way to put it. It is almost always more an act of recognition upon meeting, as if we already knew each other well, just never had a chance to meet before. Years ago, I felt the same way when I fly-fished for the first time: it was not so much I got interested in it, or hooked, or fascinated by it in some way or another. It was a dawning of recognition, beyond doubts and need to question anything: here was something I would be doing for the rest of my life. Maybe we are born as fly-fishermen or women, and it just takes us varying amounts of time to find out who we are.

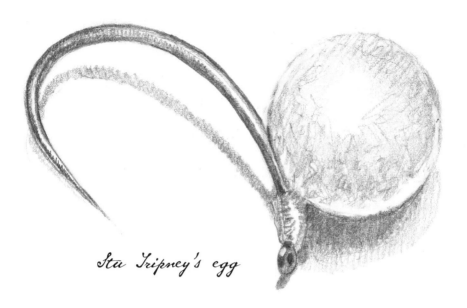

Stu Tripney's egg

When you encounter such a river friend there is an instant compatibility and much of it is beyond words. You can fish together as if you've done it many times before, in companionable silence, for similar reasons and with a concordant reverence for the trout and the wild and natural places where the fish live. This togetherness on a river somehow magnifies the experience of fishing, takes it to a level of intensity that is rarely achievable alone.

There is a loose and unassociated tribe of people from which most of my river friends come and of whom I've come to think of as the trout bohemians because of their lifestyle choices and attitudes, propensity for nomadic existence and the incomparable delight they derive from it. A common term for them would be trout bums, but to me such labelling seems trite and unjust, like calling a top brain surgeon a quack. Most of them are not bums at all. They are retired businessmen, academics on sabbaticals and off-season professional guides. I know a doctor, an aircraft engineer, a former punk rocker, a radiologist, a lawyer, a sea captain, a master-craftsman and antique dealers. They are educated, well travelled and well read, often financially independent, versed in the ways of the world and a host of other subjects. Some would make exemplary Renaissance men and women. Certainly, then, not bums.

What they do have in common, though, is that their lives and their priorities, at least for large parts of the year, have been devoted to the unwavering passion for trout. Theirs is the highest level of fly-fishing skills you'll see anywhere, yet they are often obsessive about refining them further. They share an unquenchable thirst for being with the rivers and for being in the wild often for weeks at a time, coming into towns only to resupply and do the laundry. At times, the pursuit of trout seems but an excuse for such a lifestyle.

The trout bohemians have priorities different from those of most other people, and often a different set of values, which can be at odds with those of the society. By definition, bohemianism is unconventional and nonconformist, and might even be seen as an escape from reality, if not a subscription to a different kind of reality altogether. But I'll ask you: in the world which revels in disaster and strife, where wars are made into infotainment, consumerism into a state religion, and where the only news that sells is bad news, isn't this sidetracking into the solitude of Nature and deliberate simplicity an attractive proposition?

Some of the trout bohemians are locals who had long ago realised what an amazing country they live in; others come from overseas, the way artists and writers flocked to the 1930s Paris, to indulge their passion, gypsy lifestyle and to find kindred spirits. They could go anywhere — to Alaska, Patagonia or Kamchatka — but they come here, to the Country of Trout, to what the Nelson guide Zane Mirfin called the 'last best place'. Which is why I've come to think of New Zealand as the Trout Bohemia.

I crossed the last bridge and my heart skipped a beat. The butterflies in the stomach alighted again and would not settle. I was back on my river. It meandered in easy oxbows up the long wide valley, the willows lining its banks fresh with a green haze of new leaves.

I drove upstream to reacquaint myself with the waters. I saw no parked cars, no other fly-fishers anywhere. Coming here had always felt to me like entering a rustic idyll, decades behind the rest of the world. Over the years, I fished all the beats on the river, many times over, and so a day's fishing here is for me as much alive with memories at it is with new possibilities.

Here is the place where, one evening, using a natural silk fly line I borrowed from Grandpa Trout, I caught a superb fish caddising along the high bank, while Grandpa solemnly waited for the mayfly hatch that never arose. Further up was the feed line tight against the trailing willow branches where I was spooled by a giant

I crossed the last bridge and my heart skipped a beat. The butterflies in the stomach alighted again and would not settle. I was back on my river.

trout which took my dry fly with exquisite restraint then, realising his mistake, just kept moving upstream, never running or jumping but never stopping either, pulling steadily like a draught horse, until I ran out of room to follow, ran out of the line and backing as well, until it all went slack and all I had to reel in was the algae-covered piece of a sunken willow branch.

On this river, too, I had seen the biggest mayfly hatch ever, one which could have been a highlight of any fly-fishing life but which for me turned into a pinnacle of frustration. I was guiding a lovely and enthusiastic couple who, despite their apparent passion, money, and general bon-vivant attitude for acquiring all the good experiences, dry-fly trout included, never quite cared enough to iron the kinks out their casting, not to mention taking in anything I told them about drag-free presentation.

The mega-hatch lasted for over an hour and for half of it we were fishing to one particular trout while the waters around us were literally boiling with rises. My man was casting with the vehemence of a roulette player, throw-and-hope style, his desire to engage with the trout overpowering his attention to the cast and so my dainty mayfly imitations landed anywhere, from right at our feet, on my hat and backpack, to the willow branches above the fish. All this time the trout fed voraciously, taking, it seemed, everything that floated by. Except the man's fly.

After some twenty minutes of this I lost heart and began just going through all the right motions: changing flies, smiling, offering encouragement. In similar situations, some guides would go as far as casting for their clients, passing the rod back to them for the moment of take, sometimes even after that, but

> *I just didn't have the heart to tell him the simple and honest truth, lest it may have offended. 'He won't take the bug? Too right. He hasn't seen it yet.'*

you've got to draw a line somewhere and mine was a little stern and less forgiving.

After a while an unspoken conviction must have grown in the man's mind: I didn't really know what the right fly was or didn't have the right one for the job. Finally, he voiced it.

'He won't take the bug,' he said, his hands unfolding open-palmed into the 'what's wrong' gesture.

'Fussy, i'nt he?' I said, then, drawing on all the diplomacy I could muster, added: 'Let's go and find another fish.'

I just didn't have the heart to tell him the simple and honest truth, lest it may have offended. 'He won't take the bug? Too right. He hasn't seen it yet.'

The rise eventually petered out and we went back to the motel fishless and silent. That night, by mistake or from frustration, my clients forgot to turn off their outside light. When I came back in the morning to pick them up again, the porch floor was carpeted with dead brown #16 mayflies so thick you could barely see the grey concrete beneath them. I cleared the porch, sweeping it with a broom, the way a concierge would clear the house entrance after the night's snowfall. There were so many mayflies they could have filled a bucket. I've never seen anything like this before or since.

My river of memories and promise. Two-thirds of the way up the valley I turned off the road, and through a farm gate — latched but never locked — bounced down half a mile of paddocks to another gate beyond which there were the river gravels. The farmers here are an exceptionally friendly lot. They still favour sheep over dairy cows — which in New Zealand have now become the antithesis of clean water and the bête noire of the fly-fisher

— and most of them are aware of the treasure that flows beyond their fields.

There is usually a fence between stock and the river, often an electric one and packing a solid wallop of current (I know this from direct experience) and so the sheep you see near the water are only the long-ago escapees, shaggy and wild-looking, which had evaded repeated attempts at capture and live in the no-man's-land between the farms and the river, in the impenetrable safety of the willow thicket.

I parked the camper in the shade, let out the dog, and went through the ritual of rigging up. The water is always cold here, the fish spirited, plentiful and hard to catch. A decade ago, when I first stumbled across this river I could not touch a fish for several days. It was just too hard. I stalked the banks, seeing a good number of trout, but I was unable to engage. My casts, flies, indicator, even my shadow or the shadow of my fly line, were forever spooking fish, so each day was like a long bad-luck story with many episodes compounding the effect. But I persevered because, back then, just as it is now, this seemed worth doing, a higher challenge requiring me to lift my game.

It did not come easy, but I experimented, and pondered, and drew conclusions, then discarded them and sought better ones. It was a fascinating process, a seesaw of despair and hope. Halfway through that first week I hooked my first fish here, on a single Swannundaze caddis nymph, on an extra-long and fine tippet and with no indicator, and it was an electrifying experience, if a surprise for us both. The fish threw the hook on one of its aerial somersaults, landing with a heavy splash, creating a momentary crater of white water, the line pinging back like a released rubber cord, all of this leaving me — still on my knees from the cast — trembling and in awe.

Maybe it was here that my journey of refinement began, and I'm happy that it did because good fly-fishing is largely about refinement, a progression from crude to exquisite. And maybe, a thought occurred to me as I was pulling on my waders, maybe my stalemate with Ella was a similar scenario, of skills thought considerable but proving inadequate. Maybe, I thought, she was like a river that was too hard at first but which, as its mysteries and idiosyncrasies were glimpsed and fathomed, had the power and depth to claim the most treasured place in the heart.

Maybe.

I locked Maya in the camper — this was sheep country in the middle of lambing — and approached the river. There was a tinge

THE TROUT BOHEMIA

of snow-melt in the water, but I could see into it well enough. Just up ahead was one of the best pools and, sure enough, as my eyes sharpened and the mind switched into its hunter mode, calm but alert, I immediately saw several dark smudges on the shelf where the riffle emptied into the pool. They were the colour of deep water, dark green, almost black against the golden gravel. They looked like parts of the river bed, but as I watched one of them swung across briefly, then instantly returned to its previous position. A nymphing trout.

I unhooked a tungsten-bead nymph from the rod guide-ring, essed the loose line past the rod tip and thought that, considering the fast and broken water of the riffle where I'd cast, I could probably get away with a small yarn indicator. It was always so satisfying to see the tuft of fibres, floating down innocently like a lost feather, suddenly dip under and vanish, a visual cue of imminent action, like a sharp intake of breath.

High above, invisible against the watery-blue spring sky, a skylark was chirruping its breathless song, and ahead I had miles of river to fish.

It was good to be back.

chapter 2

I think I fish, in part, because it's an antisocial, bohemian business that, when gone about properly, puts you forever outside the mainstream culture without actually landing you in an institution.'

JOHN GIERACH

If you haven't yet grasped what constitutes a trout bohemian you need to meet Jetske and Cyril. I first saw them on the bridge of the Haupiri, inland from Greymouth. After a week on my River of the Heart I had driven up the West Coast for some early-season exploration and, after a day of nosing around the spring creeks of Lake Brunner, I'd come to the Haupiri, fresh and yet unknown to me. I worked the camper down a rutted overgrown track and on to the rocky river bed until the bridge was high up above, a silhouette of struts and steel against the sky between two banks of rainforest. It was well after sundown, coming up gin o'clock, and I put a bottle of tonic in the river to cool, with the noose of a parachute cord around its neck. I anchored it to a rock, all the while scanning the feed line against the far bank, on a lookout for any rises.

The Haupiri, stained by a tributary that flows through the rainforest and thus absorbs its tannins, was running the colour of bourbon. It is a mountain river, probably not the best place for an evening rise, but you never know. If there was a fish in the long run by the camper and if it was prepared to rise, I was ready to catch it. Until the visitors showed up.

A forest-green Land Cruiser Prado with a coffin-style ski rack on its roof rolled along the bridge high above in that slow deliberate way that all fly-fishers drive across potential trout waters. Clearly, they would have seen me camping below, seen that the place was already taken, I thought, returning to my camp chores. But, no. The truck stopped in a pull-in bay just past the bridge and two figures in identical-twin outfits of waders and fishing jackets walked back on to the bridge and, leaning against the railing, began to study the water below.

They must have liked what they saw, just as I had an hour or so earlier, for they went back to their truck and returned with their rods, at the sight of which my tolerance for their company burst like a soap bubble. My own rod was leaning against the camper and my waders were hanging from the truck's snorkel. Did I also need a banner strung across the river to let them know I had every intention to fish here myself? I went up to tell them just that and more. About our fishing etiquette, about not crowding a guy but respecting his space and giving him room to fish.

Walking up, I thought that fly-fishing, and especially 'sight' fishing as we practice it in New Zealand, must be one of the most antisocial pursuits you can think of. In just about any other activity, perhaps excluding hunting, you'd welcome the fellow fiends, invite them in, swap stories, share the experiences and expertise, and maybe even conjoin in the action. But not in fly-fishing for sighted trout.

This is not about standing in the water waving a stick. To sight-fish a river you need several kilometres of undisturbed water, ideally one that has not been fished for a day or two or more, the longer the better. A sight-fisher would not consider second-hand water any more than backcountry skiers would want to ski in someone else's tracks, instead of making their own in fresh powder snow. These are refined yet also elusive qualities, not easily communicated to those who had not experienced them. If you're a sight-fishing convert you know what I'm talking about; if you're not — yet — just trust me on this one. On a river you're about to stalk for trout, your river for the duration of the fishing, even one stranger is a crowd. Two are an invasion.

The visitors excused themselves in polite Franglais, got talking and as they did all the indignation suddenly drained from me. Sure enough, from where we stood looking down on my camp I couldn't see either the rod or the waders. I took a closer look at the two anglers. Jetske's make-up was still perfect after a day's fishing. She had a warm disarming smile and Cyril's face wore a perpetual expression of a child dazed from finding too many presents under his Christmas tree. The presents, it turned out, were all trout, many of unexpectedly large size.

We camped together that night and as we talked into the late hours, and put the bottle of river-cold tonic to good use, there was that sense of recognition, that we were of the tribe. Over the days that followed, getting to know them a little better, I secretly began to wonder if perhaps, to fill in the void he had left behind, Grandpa Trout may have sent them in his stead.

They were two of the gentlest souls you'd ever meet, in such harmony with each other that much of their communication seemed almost telepathic. From October to April, their third New Zealand season now, Cyril and Jet lived in their Land Cruiser Prado which — and this was its saving grace — had that large ski box where they could put away their rods, wet waders and boots. Inside the truck, the back seats were permanently down and a plywood floor divided the space into storage and kitchen at the bottom and a mezzanine wriggle-in bedroom at the top. They only sought accommodation if they got be-stormed by a week of foul weather or if they absolutely had to go to town. The rest of the time they camped by rivers, shunning noise, civilisation and most other fly-fishers. Later, they'd even terminate their cellphone contract. They just didn't have any more use for the thing.

It was so cosy inside the Prado you could not swing a mouse in there, even the deer-hair variety, but when it rained and they were car-bound they tied flies in there, his vice secured to the bottom of the steering wheel, hers to the dashboard handle the Land Cruisers provide for bumpy off-roading.

'There are feathers everywhere, the windows get all steamed up,' Jet shrugged, then pursed her lips in that inimitable French fashion: what can you do? It was as natural as rain.

Before opting out for the trout bohemian lifestyle, they had a business together, a dealership in antique and design furniture in Geneva.

'It was like good fishing, a hunt for rare trophies,' Cyril told me, his eyes twinkling. 'We would do research and reconnaissance, find the best and rarest pieces, try to buy them, bring them home.'

They would do thousands of kilometres driving the countryside, following leads. It was a treasure hunt and they got used to living out of a truck. Somewhere along the way of the twenty-plus years' marriage Cyril introduced Jet to fly-fishing, and it was like falling in love all over again. They began taking road trips into the Lozère region near Massif Central in south-eastern France, a place of peaty rivers, hard granite landscapes and small but hellishly difficult trout. They showed me photos of their home waters there: streams you could jump across, trout that fitted into the palms of both hands put together, with neither head nor tail protruding beyond that.

Those trips got longer and longer, until they decided to spend an entire trout season there. It was a turning point for them, a re-evaluation of life's priorities.

'We thought: do we keep working eighty-hour weeks, getting stressed up and paying more and more taxes, snatching a free weekend now and then, or do we just stop this insanity and do what we love most, do what we always wanted to do?' Cyril told me as the dinner wine loosened his tongue.

'Hmm, that'd be a tough call to make,' I said, and we all laughed. Jet shrugged.

'Chez nous, we'd be considered losers for giving up the business life just when the going was good. But who cares what others think? Why would you want all their fancy stuff — the latest cars, and gadgets and designer everything — if you can have this?' She nodded towards the river.

We were sitting on our foldable camping chairs, the water murmuring past. My hurricane lamp doubled as a campfire because all driftwood was too wet to light, and nearby Maya was chewing on a bone with her usual single-minded determination, gristle crunching in those hyena jaws. In a silent lull that followed the conversation, when all that was important was already said and the trivial wasn't worth bringing up, I watched my new friends with wonder and a twinge of jealousy. They were so profoundly content with each other, so enchanted by the rivers and the trout that they didn't seem to need anyone or anything else.

'On est les solitaires a deux,' Jet would tell me later.

Solitary in togetherness, together in their solitude. I never thought such a state was possible. Just being with those two was like sitting by a good fire.

It warmed your heart.

The following morning we fished the Haupiri together, upstream from the bridge and through the land of the Christian community which established an industrious if somewhat introverted existence here some two decades ago. It was around that time that the community founder and its charismatic evangelical leader was charged and imprisoned for several sexual assaults involving girls as young as twelve and a wooden object. I didn't share this piece of local lore with Cyril and Jet, unsure if they'd really want to know it.

Occasionally, we got glimpses of Amish-like outfits and averted faces, women in white headscarves, and long, navy-blue dresses, men also in blue — dark trousers, lighter shirts — each with the garrotte of a black tie. Identical haircuts, indistinguishable faces, uniformed sameness all around. The antithesis of bohemia.

The river was bouldery and clear, and beyond the tributary much smaller and no longer tinged with the forest tannins. Jet again looked as if she'd stepped freshly out of a cosmetics ad, carrying nothing but her rod and an ammo belt loaded with fly boxes, while Cyril burdened himself with a massive bum-bag full of gear and a landing net with a gape the size of a child's hula hoop. Not here to catch sprats, that much was certain.

'Our season's trophy in the Lozère was a brown trout of one and a half pounds,' Cyril confessed when I ribbed him about the size of the net. 'Jet's first fish in New Zealand was over ten pounds. It was quite a shock. We almost lost it. Didn't have a net big enough to land it.'

He hefted the handle of his net.

'This is a salmon net. Perfect for the size of trout we've been catching.'

Jet was at the point, moving like a lioness on a hunt, threading her way through giant thistles that had overgrown the high stopbank, eyes focused on the river, body frequently freezing mid-step, senses alert, movements silent.

'Ah!' she paused again and with deliberate slowness lowered herself into a crouch.

'Voila, une belle,' she whispered reverently, her finger pointing to the fish.

Peering over her shoulder and sighting down her outstretched arm I also saw the trout, hovering partway off the bottom in a trough between two large brown boulders. It was feeding with abandon, its sinuous body swaying in the fast current of the trough which must have been funnelling food straight to it.

'Your turn,' Cyril said to me with an eager nod towards the fish.

'Jet, why don't you have a go?' I tried protesting, but she was already shaking her head.

'Non, non, non, non, non! You fish. We watch,' she said, making herself comfortable on the ground, with Cyril crouching next to her. From up here, they had ringside seats for what was about to follow.

We were nearly on top of the fish and I had to backtrack downstream for a less conspicuous place to cast.

There is something else you need to know about these two. I've never seen fly-fishing so pure as the way they practise it. Sight-fishing only, never a blind cast. Natural silk lines for dry fly, no indicators for nymphs. They walked the banks together slowly; in the water they moved with such measured pace they made no wake or waves that could alert fish to their presence. In this promised land of trout they found in New Zealand, they took delight in every opportunity, every metre of a riverbank, often focusing on the water more difficult to see into, the fast runs and the pockets.

'On some of the popular trophy rivers everyone is just running from pool to pool because it's easy to see the fish in there,' Cyril said. 'But, remember, the easier the fish is to see, the harder it is to catch. We've had fabulous fishing in the faster water other people have skipped. You just have to walk more slowly and look harder.'

We were on the high bank, its riverside face an eroding slope of gravel, with big round stones cemented within it, but coming loose underfoot. Climbing down, I cringed as couple of fist-sized rocks tumbled down and splashed into the water.

'He still there?' I asked my companions.

'Oui,' they answered in duet harmony.

'Still feeding,' Cyril added.

At last I was down on the waterline and not making any more clumsy noises. My fish was harder to see from here. Sometimes a clear window of visibility passed over it, but mostly the trout was a shimmering blur, easily mistaken for a play of current over rocks. At any other time, by default, I would use an indicator, but with these two the rules of engagement were strict and clearly defined.

'Would it bother you if I used an indicator?' Still, it was worth a try.

'Oui,' again the two voices answered in unison.

'It would?'

'Certainly,' said Cyril. 'You'll see the fish take. What you need an indicator for?'

It was a one-cast job, lobbing the heavy tungsten stonefly a good few metres above the trough, and the plop of the nymph was disguised in the turbulent water there. Stripping the line to keep up with the current, I strained to see the fish, saw it sway to the side, thought it took the fly, doubted it, felt an angry weight of the trout briefly, then felt my line tear out of the water on recoil, knotting itself into a gorse bush behind me.

'He still there?' I asked again. Stranger things have happened.

'Non, he's gone,' Cyril stood up and stretched his back.

I untangled and caught up with them.

Jet made a sad consolatory face and said 'Oh! Quelle dommage.' What a pity. Then she giggled, shrugged and took up the point again.

Pity indeed, I thought. With an indicator, I would have got that fish. It was deep in the water, and despite that it looked big. It could have been one of my season's trophies, certainly a good fit for Cyril's hula-hoop net. Alas, for now, it was: trout one; purism nil. With those two, though, it would not stay that way for long.

Sure enough, not fifty metres upstream I heard Jet take a sharp breath and saw her point again to something in the water below. As if on command, we all dropped to our knees. And this was how one of the Christian farmers found us. He must have come to check what the three strangers were up to wandering through their land, for he poked his head over the rise of the stopbank and stared at us for a long while. But we were no threat to their peace and privacy.

Seeing us down on our knees, facing the river in reverence, perhaps he thought we too were praying.

Long before Bohemia became a concept, a state of mind and a way of being, it existed as a geographical region, a kingdom encompassing what these days is the western part of the Czech Republic. I used to rock-climb there as a young man, when I still thought the meaning of life was to be found in climbing mountains and crags, claiming the conquest only to climb down again, a process, you notice, much like catch and release.

Today, a nostalgic relic of that long-gone kingdom is the Duchy of Bohemia, which still maintains the sovereign status of a micro-nation and a government-in-exile unrecognised by anyone but themselves. Its seat and land holdings are a long way from home though, in Nevada, USA.

What gave birth to the name bohemian was a case of mistaken identity. When the Roma people, commonly known as gypsies, first arrived in France around the fifteenth century, they were thought to have come from Bohemia and so they were called the bohemians, and for a long time the label implied rather unsavoury qualities. Bohemians were considered riff-raff: dirty, vagrant, neither employed nor employable, contrarians to the values of society, dismissive of its conformism, untroubled by its disapproval, a threat to the status quo.

You could see how the idea of seceding from conventional life, of being a fringe-dweller with unorthodox and anti-establishment ideas, would be instantly attractive to artists, writers, musicians and other free-thinkers already at odds with the restrictions and expectations of society. By definition, being a bohemian entailed poverty, voluntary or otherwise, but, as Pablo Picasso suggested, there were ways around this particular hurdle. He wrote: 'I wish I could live like a poor man, but with a lot of money.'

With such endorsements, it wasn't long before bohemianism became a counter-culture, a snowballing movement. Wherever it flared up — in Montmartre and Montparnasse of Paris, Fitzrovia and Soho in London, in New York's Greenwich Village — it became an enduring trend. Puccini wrote an opera about it, 'La Bohème', one of the most frequently staged shows of all time, and cultural luminaries like Paul Gauguin, Salvador Dalí and literary hotheads like Allen Ginsberg and Jack Kerouac either subscribed to the tenets of bohemianism or indeed defined them.

So what's it all got to do with fly-fishing for trout? Jet brought it home for me one night as we were all crammed into my camper: three tired anglers and one very wet dog. We got rained out of the Haupiri and while the world outside was grey and dark, inside we had a bottle of wine and beeswax candles, plenty of river stories and plans of future adventures.

'For us,' Jet said, 'New Zealand is a dream come true, the trout Bohemia.'

And I thought: 'She is right. Look at us! We *are* the trout bohemians.'

We are the trout nomads, living simply and without pretension, following our dreams and wanting to be left alone to do just that. We are happy to forgo the trappings and comforts of society so that we can indulge our true passion, engaging with the world of trout on all levels, finding joy in every fish as if it was the first one. Or the last.

We travel with purpose, pursuing this miracle of a fish that is at once the reason, an excuse and a metaphor for a larger quest. Paul Gauguin gave up a promising career as a banker to paint in the South Pacific and to live in a thatched hut. Cyril and Jet had forsaken a thriving business to live out their dream, pursue their own art.

'Travel, leave everything, follow the birds,' wrote flag-bearer bohemian Gustave Flaubert. It seemed we were doing just that, except that we were following trout.

Of course, since the time of the first bohemians such apparently idle vagrancy has not only been frowned upon, it has been actively discouraged.

'Did you know that recently legislation was passed in New Zealand which tries to make freedom camping such as this illegal?' I asked my companions.

Cyril pursed his lips, letting the air out with a derisive hiss.

'I wonder if any of the politicians have ever been camping themselves,' he said.

I wondered the same thing. Probably not. Out here, they could get their suits soiled, their limos dinged up. But, then again, trying to prohibit freedom camping, passed under parliamentary urgency and without any real public consultation, was not really about camping but about freedom. It was like treating a headache with a guillotine when all that was really needed was a lot more camp shovels and a new print run of Kathleen Meyer's timeless classic *How to Shit in the Woods*. But perhaps none of the politicians have ever done that either.

'If the governments have it their way, soon we'll all need a licence to breathe, huh?' Cyril said, and we laughed. This much was clear: the bohemians, trout or otherwise, will not be applying for that one. We are not rebels, but not conformists either because in bohemia there are no roads and you have to find your own path and navigate it with your own inner compass. With that comes the responsibility for not getting lost or waylaid. It is a fair price.

After the rain we went back to the spring creeks near Lake

Brunner which Cyril and Jet already knew better than me. The creeks are hard to fish. They run deep and the bush encroaches on them from both sides, often meeting overhead to form stretches of tunnels, gloomy and constricting. But the fresh had improved our odds, adding the slightest tincture of colour to water which is usually clear as kirsch. It had also animated the trout, and in the evenings they were rising freely among the weed beds, taking #16 CDC emergers without too many refusals. Bending down and looking upstream along the surface of the creek you could just see the mayflies struggling through the water film, drying and flexing their wings as they bobbed on the current towards us. Backlit by the evening half-light, the wings shone with delicate copper and gold, miniature candle flames snuffed out with deadly accuracy by the rising trout.

We could fish only one at a time and it was a fine arrangement. I stood waist-deep in the water, feeling the tendrils of the underwater plants sway against my legs, watching Cyril midstream, casting a silk fly line with a six-metre leader. The line landed on the water like the thread of spider web, while peering from behind the cover of bankside shrubs above us Jet offered directions.

'More to the right. Oui. Still there. Ah, he's gone.'

We took turns at rising fish, catching some, not catching others, and it didn't seem to matter who was doing the fishing and who was the spectator. I could not get enough of being with those two, of stalking the riverbanks with them, watching them hold hands on every river crossing, cooking meals together, talking long into the night. Too often, it seems, hunting for trout we get so focused on the pursuit and its results we forget to zoom out and to take in the larger view of it all, like the camaraderie of the people we are with.

In case of Cyril and Jet, bohémie and bonhomie seemed interchangeable terms.

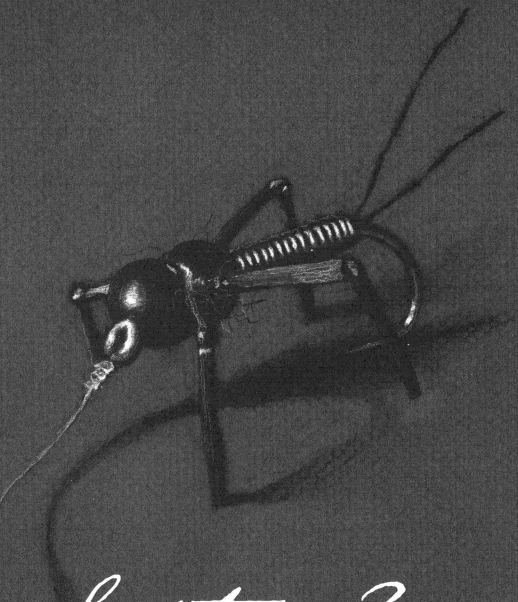

chapter 3

'I couldn't live in New Zealand. I'd just fish, fish
and fish every day. I'd never get anything else done.'

PJ JACOBS

From Lake Brunner I drove on inland, taking the back road via Nelson Creek, turning right towards Reefton. The rivers along the way were still in flood, though starting to drop already and promising to come right in a day or two, but meanwhile I rolled on in the camper looking at different waters. I've always found fly-fishing a good and easy way to travel, the quest for new places as engaging as the casting of flies itself.

The pursuit of trout is not only a reason and an excuse to explore the country; it also grants you a certain diplomatic immunity, the fly rod being both a kind of passport and a mark of harmless eccentricity that allows you to nose about, ask questions, get lost and found, search for new ways in, out and around places. You can knock on doors, seek information, ask for help, and it's all perfectly justifiable. You are, after all, on a sacred journey, a pilgrimage of your own design, meaningful only to you but respected even by those who may not understand it.

As a fly-fisher, you are no threat to anyone — sometimes, it seems, not even to the fish — but your motivation is innocent and pure, almost noble. You are on a mission, a vision quest, even if, on the surface of things, the idea of spending so much time, money and effort on catching fish only to put them back in the water makes no sense at all. The rest of the populace, though they may never pick up a rod themselves, somehow innately know that what you are doing is important. And so they often welcome you as they would a pilgrim, shower you with hospitality and insights, at the same time respecting your need for solitude and space. It is as if they understand that a fly-fisher is a soul wandering in search of itself and any finding must be accomplished first-hand and through direct experience.

Some of my most treasured adventures, encounters and friendships came to me by the way of fly-fishing and they are the trophies of a lifetime, more memorable than any fish could ever be. Take Caveman, for example. I would never have met him if I wasn't a wandering soul looking for good new dry-fly water on the Buller River, above its Upper Gorge near Murchison.

The 169-kilometre Buller is a magnificent river, wild and unmodified, running the colour of greenstone through gorges and beech forest. Its tributaries penetrate deep into three national parks — Paparoa, Kahurangi and Nelson Lakes — but the Buller itself is short, swift and muscular, a narrow end of a funnel draining over 6000 square kilometres of wilderness. The two gorges that make up both ends of that funnel occasionally overflow in cataclysmic floods. In the place known as the Hawk's Crag,

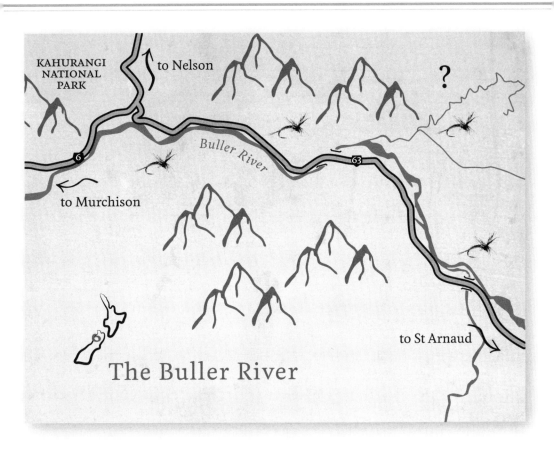

The Buller River

where the one-lane corniche cuts into the vertical wall of rock,
and the river makes an omega-shaped turn banking up against it,
an old twenty-cent coin, painted red and nailed to a weathered
wooden pole, pinpoints the high water mark of the record 1988
flood. The coin is two metres above the road and the road another
fifteen metres above the river.

It was in the gorges of the Buller that the New Zealand
equivalent of 'the worst journey in the world' took place when
the country was still a blank on the map, beyond the few dots
of coastal settlements. In 1846, unemployed surveyor Thomas
Brunner, accompanied by two Maori guides and their wives, set
out from Nelson in search of the much-rumoured great pastures
of the interior. In late December, they reached the source of
the Buller, at Lake Rotoiti. From there, they followed the river
down. First along the easy flats to the Four Rivers plains, near
today's Murchison, and on through the contorted Upper Gorge
to the confluence with the Inangahua, then along the Lower
Gorge to a deserted Maori pa on the coast. Turning south,

they went as far as Lake Paringa near Haast, before turning back. The eighteen-month-long expedition was proclaimed a failure because they never found the utopian prairies, only steep mountains, swamps and glacial rivers of uncommon severity. But their account of traversing the Buller can make the hardiest explorer wince with empathy.

Torrential rain, floods and scarcity of food turned their adventure into a do-or-die fight against the river that just wouldn't let up. They needed some 170 days — an average of a kilometre a day — to reach the sea. Brunner wrote: 'I am getting so sick of this exploring, the walking and the diet being both so bad, that were it not for the shame of the thing, I would return to the more comfortable quarters of the Riwaka Valley.'

The rest of his diary entries are a crescendo of despair and failing hope:

3 March: 'Continued rain [. . .] fern root served out in small quantities twice a day. This is without exception the very worst country I have ever seen in New Zealand; not a bird to be had or seen.'
13 March: 'We all passed a most miserable night, not having room either to lie down or sit up, and the women moaning with pain.'
14 March: 'Our fern root almost exhausted, and no food to be found.'
21 March: 'Rain continuing, dietary shorter, strength decreasing, spirits failing, prospects fearful.'

There were no trout in the river back then so fishing wasn't a viable option either. Two months later, within a day's walk from the coast, they were forced to eat their dog Rover, the beast itself already a starved bag of bones.

Today you can drive Brunner's three-month epic in about two hours, although from the comfortable highway you get only glimpses of the river. There are trout — muscular and spirited like the river itself — throughout the Buller now, but the best fly water is up above the gorges, upstream from Murchison, and this is where I always go.

If I'm a little sentimental about the Buller, I have my reasons. It was here, along the stretches of the upper river, that I learnt to fly-fish, or at least took a most significant step in my evolution as an angler. Years ago, I was on a magazine assignment here and a part of it involved going for a fish with Zane Mirfin, a young guide with a degree in trout management, under the wings of legendary Tony

Entwistle and already something of a local angling prodigy. By that time, I'd already fished a good deal, but catching trout still seemed more a matter of luck than skills or understanding.

We walked up to the river across a paddock as long and flat as an airport runway, and on the bank Zane tied on a heavy caddis nymph and a tuft of yarn for an indicator. He cast that into the eye of the nearest pool and — bang! — had a fish just like that, on his first cast.

Like the river, the trout was magnificent, the colour of greenstone and just as cold but alive like a flame. At the time, catching a fish was always the event of a day for me, and not every day either, and so all this — casually walking up to a river, catching a 4-lb trout with the first cast — seemed something of a miracle, a magician's trick. You could easily dismiss it for a stroke of luck were it not for the fact that Zane repeated it several times that day, each time with equal ease and nonchalance.

He made me catch fish too, turning our outing into my best river day to date, and that despite the squalls of rain that lashed us without respite. The strangest thing was that, when I went back to the river the next day, alone and trying to recapture and repeat some of that magic, I managed to do just that and more. I hooked several good fish, a definite first for me those days, and landed most of them, including a beauty of over 6 lbs, the biggest trout I'd caught until then. If the river ran through this land like a vein of liquid greenstone, the varieties of New Zealand jade — the speckled kokopu of the gravel-bed shallows, the light-green translucent kahurangi of the clearest pools, the milky colour of inanga of a river in flood — were all present in the camouflage of that trout. There were flecks of gold in the trout's skin patterns too, and so each fish was like a gem extracted from the green depths, to be admired briefly, returned and remembered.

Then, just as I thought this was again my best day ever, there was an evening rise, short but explosive. The deep green waters of the Buller are hard to see into and so much of the time the river may appear fishless. Now, seeing a dozen or so fish slurping mayflies, breaking the surface with so much punch each rise left a starburst of white water, well, I just fell apart at the sight of all that. My hands shook so hard I could barely change a fly. It was like trying to thread a needle in a sewing machine while the motor was still running.

Maybe evolution is not linear, maybe it proceeds in quantum leaps once enough momentum is gathered, but from that day on I started to catch fish with a degree of consistency. The days of 'chuck and chance', of hoping against impossible odds, were gone forever.

When I went out now I began expecting to catch fish, and most of
the times I did. Things would happen: fish sightings, hook-ups,
landings won and lost, trophies or tiddlers, but always something,
some action or adventure, an engagement with the trout. With that
came confidence, which led to more frequent engagements and
from there the journey of refinement began. That day I crossed
some invisible threshold of initiation, became a fly-fisherman,
stopped being a wannabe. It was like learning to swim, not the going
through the biomechanics of it all, the coordination and breathing,
but reaching the point when you stop fighting the water, when
you feel that it'll support you and you can relax into it, and that,
barring any extreme circumstances, you will never drown of your
own accord. All that happened for me on the Buller, which is why I
had been coming back to the river at every opportunity.

This time too, I was driving up the river looking for some fresh
dry-fly water. I wanted something harder to access and thus not
frequented by the drive-by angling crowd, a place I had not yet
explored, and I was told a fellow named Evans would be the best
source of such information. Apparently, he worked on the river,
knew it well, and he could point me to all the right places.

Problem was the man himself seemed impossible to find.

In Murchison again, I drove around asking about him but
no one, not even, as it turned out, his closest neighbour, could
tell me who and where he was. I asked two men repairing an old
Bedford truck, a rust bucket that looked freshly salvaged from a
West Coast swamp, and they replied with blank stares.

'Evans. You know, the gold diver?' I persisted.

'Ah, Caveman!' one of them lit up. 'Sure, we know Caveman.
He's in that house next door.'

The house looked old, almost derelict, and outside the
backdoor there was a picnic table turned into a work-bench and
the tools lay scattered everywhere. In the living room lit by the
morning TV, Caveman's partner Teresa was finishing a piece of
mail-order needlework and her daughter Bonnie was playing
with an empty bird's nest, woven tightly like a tiny wicker basket.
Caveman himself — his children call him Cavie — was a wild-
looking man with a Moses beard and an air of bikie 'been to hell
and back' past that was best left undisturbed. His friend would later
tell me that, in the roller-coaster of life, Cavie got down so low,
the only way was either up or out. He came up, a changed man.

Over endless brews of weak instant coffee, he told me of his days
as a professional hunter, trapping possums, shooting deer and pigs
for a government culler's wage. But the hunting days were over and

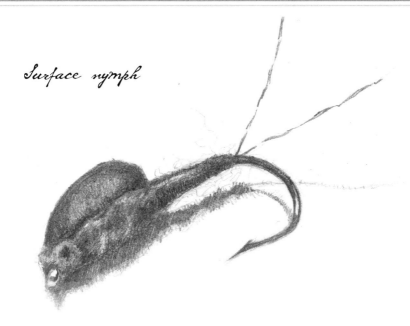

Surface nymph

now he made his living by diving for gold along the bottom of the Buller. After the recent rain and a minor flood, his dredge needed refloating and I offered to help. From Cavie's description, it was clear his dredge was not far from the general area I wanted to fish.

We drove to the river and lowered the dredge on ropes down a steep eroded bank. There was no white water here, just swift smooth current, sinewy and unrelenting. The dredge was an alloy frame bolted atop four plastic floats, two motors on one end, a trough lined with wire mesh running lengthwise through the middle. With its long trunk of the suction hose probing the bottom, the whole apparatus resembled a caricature elephant, tethered in the current.

Cavie pulled on his black wetsuit. The tight hood, heavy articulated weight belt and his long greying beard made him look like a Templar knight. He fired up the motors, one of which powered the air compressor. Two long yellow hoses led to his backpack, one was the airline, the other constantly injected his wetsuit with warm water, preventing him from sure hypothermia. As he stood chest-deep in the river, a bow wave of white water foamed around him. The motor's exhaust pipe spewed blue-grey fumes in his face, blowing away the mob of sandflies. The noise of engines was deafening, the only way of communication an improvised sign language.

Cavie dived in and began vacuuming the river bed. The stream of fine gravel poured over the mesh trays and a fan of muddy tailings formed behind the dredge. 'That's the end of fishing,' I thought to myself. The noise and the muck would have cleared the river of trout a mile in each direction.

An hour passed. A red Incept raft loaded with adventure tourists shot by on its way down the gorge, the punters yahooing and saluting with their paddles, the guide giving the dredge a wide berth. On the surface, regular bursts of air bubbles measured out Cavie's 'bottom time'. Standing on the bank, I synchronised my own breathing with the frequency of fizzing bubbles. Cavie's breathing was short and laboured, the breath of a mountain runner climbing a steep hill.

'Wanna have a go?' Cavie asked after he emerged from his stint under water. Despite the wetsuit and the heating system he was shivering hard, his lips blue and numb, a red bug-eye shape of the mask imprinted on his face.

Sure, I thought. I was here to fish, but why not? Regardless of gold, it would be interesting to see where the trout live, beyond the surface veil that separates their world from ours like a flexing mirror.

With Cavie's spare wetsuit on and the rest of his diving gear I waded into the river, which any bushcraft instructor would surely pronounce unfordable. Holding on to the branches of sunken trees, I dropped to the bottom where the current was less strong and crept upstream towards the nozzle, reaching from one rocky handhold to another, as if climbing up the face of a waterfall.

How could trout live against such force?

At the end of the hose I set to work. Like a portable black hole, the fifteen-centimetre-wide nozzle sucked in the rocks and gravels embedded in silt, until solid river bed was showing. Stones the size of oranges disappeared down the suction tube. Cavie told me that he would move a truckload of gravel in a day's work. That could produce up to two ounces of gold. And the gold was here, alright. On the yet-undisturbed bottom, specks of golden dust glittered like brocade.

My gold fever did not persist. The water was cold with snowmelt and within minutes I was losing feeling in my face and hands. As I followed the underwater handrails of branches and stumps back to the surface, I couldn't help but admit that this man Cavie, a self-taught diver who built all his equipment by gutsy trial and costly error deserved every grain of colour he found.

With the price of gold at the record high and only going up, Cavie's venture would seem lucrative, were it not for the other, unpredictable side to it: the whims and moods of the river.

'Floods are my biggest worry,' he said. 'When it rains hard, I can't sleep. I often come here, with a spotlight, to check on the river and the dredge. My entire livelihood could be flushed away at any time.'

Once, at midnight, the river was at its normal flow, but by 7 a.m., it rose ten metres and, when it eventually subsided, it left the dredge stranded six metres up a tree. You quickly learn to respect the river, Cavie said, you have to otherwise you won't live to have another lesson. Many times he found himself outwrestled by the current, hanging on for dear life at the end of his air hose, downstream of the dredge. Just below his claim, the river enters the Upper Gorge and cascades down in a series of white-water rapids. Good spot for rafting but no place for a swimmer.

Despite the dangers, Cavie had no intentions of quitting, perhaps because after so many hours and days spent with the river he had learnt its ways, felt its powerful current in his own veins. As a parting gift, he told me a good place to fish upstream from where he worked, and gave me a sliver of gold I had dredged up, bright but tiny like a grain of rice.

An amulet for the Buller, the river of gold and greenstone trout.

There was a shy evening rise that night in a pool above Cavie's claim, but the first trout I hooked on a drab parachute dry with a hi-vis post charged upstream, knocking four or five other fish from their feeding stations before throwing the hook on a jump. After that, the pool went dead quiet. I was hemmed in by cliffs, with no alternative water below, and so for a while I watched the mayflies as they continued to hatch, unmolested by trout. They drifted down on veinlets of current, bobbing and spinning as they clambered out of their nymphal shucks, pushing down with their legs as if squeezing through a hatchway between two worlds. Briefly, they dried their wings, a phenomenon not unlike the blossoming of a flower, then took off in hyperbolic flight paths into a life that was as mysterious as it was ephemeral.

For long minutes not one trout nose appeared from below to interrupt the spectacle, but as the twilight came on small dimples began to appear on the river's surface. I felt a surge of hope, then realised what it was: the mock rises were caused by droplets of rain, fat and boisterous. Next, the entire river surface had gone matt and opaque, churned into a sheet of white water from the pummelling of rain. We ran for the camper, Maya barking and leaping around as if it was some kind of a game, me muttering curses about the weather.

This sonofabitch rain had been following us all the way up the Coast, a spoilsport intent on flushing us out of one good place to another, only to catch us up again once we got there. Sure enough, it poured all night, the beating of rain against the camper's fibreglass canopy so loud it was hard to sleep for the noise. In the morning the grass bank where I had parked was a saturated sponge and the river was high and fast, and rising still. There was nothing for it but to keep heading east, past the source of the Buller near St Arnaud, down the plains of the Wairau River, and into Marlborough.

Such is the nature of New Zealand, its compactness and geographical extremes, you can drive from a flood and into a drought within an hour or less. Just reaching the Wairau where it comes out of the Rainbow Valley and turns east towards the Pacific, we had outrun the rain and minutes later we were back in sunshine. Although it was still late spring, Marlborough was already dry. There were only two colours in the landscape: the azure blue of an empty sky and the straw yellow of sunburnt grass.

The grass was scorched stiff and it crunched underfoot like cornflakes; the sheep I saw stood motionless, overheating in their dusty coats, studying the pools of their own shadows. Looking back west from where we came I could not see the mountains. They were still swallowed up by the apocalyptic storm, black clouds pouring over their crests. The clouds miraculously stopped partway down the slope, melting away, not making it any further.

What did come down, though, gaining strength as it did so, was the wind. The kind that can rip the doors off your truck or prevent you from opening them, depending on which angle to it you park. It was the relentless nor'wester, with all its moisture filtered by the mountains. It's a wind that saps your energy, makes you feel dejected and irritable. It parches the land and drives twisters of dust, dribbling crumpled junk mail along deserted roads.

I nosed the camper down a river access track, let out the dog and took stock of the prospects. The Wairau is entirely different from the Buller, flowing wide and braided without any constrictions or gorges. Spotting fish is difficult here as the background is limited only to stands of willows and the rest of the water is notoriously glary, but there are runs of good structure and

This sonofabitch rain had been following us all the way up the Coast, a spoilsport intent on flushing us out of one good place to another, only to catch us up again once we got there.

long glides where the surface has a smooth metallic sheen on which rises show as crisp as engravings.

But not today. The pools downstream from me had whitecaps on them as far as I could see, and looking up was like staring into the vent of a sandblaster. Anything hatching in this wind was not likely to stop before it hit the coast of Chile. I briefly contemplated fishing downstream — it was probably feasible, if only just — but, well, after the finesse of fishing with Cyril and Jet, after watching the spring-creek trout sip tiny emergers and trying to cast to them with exquisite precision, pulling a Woolly Bugger through choppy waters in a howling wind felt crude and unengaging, and more than a little desperate.

'Forget the fishing,' I said to Maya, noticing that she too was sheltering in the lee of the camper. 'Let's go and reconnoitre some more access points for later.'

I drove down the road which paralleled the river, exploring every potential access along the way, mapping them in my road atlas. There was a lot of good water, if only this wind would let up.

Along one of the dirt lanes I saw a farmer riding astride a quad bike. He was towing a long plume of dust, heading for an enclosure that looked like something out of Jurassic Park.

The fishing was a total non-event but how about getting some fine fly-tying material instead? I followed the man down the driveway, met him and stated my business.

'Sure,' he said, unlocking the gate.

At the sound of that and no doubt the sight of the man too — it must have been about feeding time — a mob of ostriches blew in from the paddock, black stately bodies afloat long and scaly saurian legs, their stunning feathers fluffed up and dishevelled by the gale. They crowded around us, cocking their heads, craning their hairy, pipe-like necks, snapping with their beaks. This snapping, the farmer whose name was Shaun explained, was an act of friendly curiosity, the equivalent of a dog sniffing a stranger, although it felt more like being probed for tenderness with a pair of wide-nosed pliers.

Ostriches are instantly likeable, goofy, industrial-strength birds that could peck you to death out of sheer destructive curiosity — the way children hack apart a mechanical toy just to see what's inside. You buy a cute little chick with furry kiwi-like feathers, Shaun said, and in twenty-four months it grows into a 2.5-metre-tall cross between a turkey and a giraffe.

'How many feathers you want?' he asked.

'Half a dozen would last me a lifetime,' I said, and running his fingers like a comb through the birds' rumps Shaun plucked several quills, the herls along their length drooping languidly, soft and pliable. The big birds pecked at him, but he elbowed their necks out of the way.

'It's the legs you've got to watch out for,' he said. 'Get close enough and they can't kick you.'

Ostrich herl is a superb tying material, with some of the characteristics of CDC. It gets wet well, and it sheds water with equal ease. It does not float, of course, but it's much more durable than peacock, versatile and easy to work with, lifelike, and particularly good for bodies and heads. You'll find it commercially dyed into many colours. Mine were only white, but they were also fresh and unadulterated. Still warm. If tied on sparsely, I thought, and especially when seen as a silhouette, they may just add the right amount of semi-translucent fuzziness which implies moving limbs of an insect.

It seemed I was as fascinated with my new herl as Shaun was with his ostriches.

'Great beasts for this arid climate, they are,' he enthused, 'practical, too. Very little wastage.'

There was hardly a part of an ostrich that could not be turned into something useful and usually expensive. Skin for Gucci leather handbags. Oil for cosmetics. Eyelashes for painters' brushes. Ground toenails for — what else? — Oriental aphrodisiacs. But most of all, it was the lean, low-cholesterol meat which, Shaun assured me, tasted better than any cut of beef.

What if the ostriches should break out and go feral, I asked.

Should we rekindle the moa ovens?

Shaun laughed. 'Ostriches would never run away. They're too curious. They follow you around like a pack of dogs.'

I thanked him for the feathers and drove on. Like any waterway used extensively for irrigation, the Wairau is a curious kind of river: the further downstream you go, the less water seems to be flowing in its gravel bed. This wide valley, walled in by the imposing Richmond Range in the north and the aptly named Wither Hills in the south, was once classic sheep country, tranquil and rustic, but today much of it is devoted to making internationally renowned white wines, most notably its sauvignon blanc. Vineyards as far as the eye can see. Even the river disappears among them.

There is a self-assured nobility in the way these vines grow, how the gnarled branches lean on their treillage like an old wise man bracing on his staff. Watching them, vivid green in the arid landscape, is to witness a small miracle that something so good and ancient can thrive in the shallow, stony soil.

But even the hardiest of plants — vines and the pine trees which cover the Richmond Range — need water, and while the ranges snag their own weather, and rain, the vines in the valley have to be irrigated. Considering their untold numbers this requires a vast amount of water. Trout water. Little wonder the river gets thinner the further down it flows.

With my fishing turning from great expectations to gone with the wind I kept driving down the valley. The region was on the verge of another drought. There had been no significant rain for weeks and where the tributary creeks once ran, the bridges now spanned troughs of sun-baked gravel. The weather forecasters publicly apologised for using an expression 'the risk of showers', even though they still ended their prognostications with the unchanging 'and for Marlborough, fine and dry'. They didn't need to add: and windy like a s.o.b.

Within a few weeks the Fish & Game rangers, helped by volunteers, would be rescuing trout stranded in pools disconnected from the main river.

Water, water, precious water. There was not enough of it to go around for all who needed it.

After a charged and eventful start, the magic of my heart river and the days with Cyril and Jet, my bohemian trout trip was losing its momentum. I could have put it down to weather: rain in the west, the howler wind in the east. The wind especially would make a good scapegoat. After all, it was the New Zealand scientist Neil Cherry who showed that the nor'wester had deep psychological effects on many people, apparently due to upsetting the melatonin—serotonin balance in the body. Those affected felt they couldn't cope with everyday things, experienced irrational anxieties and a sense of foreboding.

But it wasn't that. This time around, though quite extreme, the weather and the state of rivers were only of peripheral importance to me. My camper, which I had furnished into a veritable trout-mobile, offers many diversions. A full fly-tying kit equipped with Marc Petitjean tools. Wi-Fi with cellular broadband. A year's worth of reading, both in my bulging book bag and the iPad library. Music, movies, work, a minibar. A box of exercise gear. With this kind of back-up I always felt I could hole up anywhere, weather any storm.

This time, however, all the stuff seemed irrelevant. With growing certainty I realised just how much I was missing Ella. I felt lonely without her, and I'd rarely been lonely before. It had been over three weeks and we had not exchanged one communication — not a text, email or voice message.

I was missing our dinners and coffees, the long mountain-bike rides along the river trails, the talks about art and the nature of creativity. I was missing her graceful ways, her easy laughter, her delightful English accent and the deadpan wit, always barbless but sharp and keen as Mustad.

The first time we went on an overnight fishing trip together, still in the bright glow of the honeymoon when we could do no wrong, we looked for a river access and stopped to ask a farmer. To our surprise — for in New Zealand such behaviour is a rarity — the grumpy old man was openly unfriendly, if not outright hostile.

'Mind if we fish here?' Ella asked, putting on her most charming smile.

'You can't,' the man blurted out.

'Mate,' she replied without missing a beat, 'even if you don't want us here, there is no need to use obscenities. Or call us names.'

The man's face furrowed with effort and puzzlement. Puns were obviously not his forte.

Now, remembering all this in the camper, nudged into a windbreak of willows as the twilight descended on the river and the wind eased into a zephyr as it often does after sundown, I wondered I had made a terrible mistake. Maybe I shouldn't have left the way I did. The reasons for bailing out were valid then, but now they suddenly seemed trivial. In fact, I already found it hard to remember them clearly. I'd just run away again, as I did so often in the past when things got too difficult.

Yet deep inside I aspired to the very opposite. My role models were those who stayed, who worked things out and grew stronger and closer to each other by doing so. But how did they do it? Were Cyril and Jet just lucky or did they know something I didn't, a secret to staying together no matter what came their way? And they were not the only ones.

A couple of years earlier, while snooping around the Upper Grey, I saw a Land Cruiser camper like mine, parked by the river. They are exceptionally rare in this country and I stopped to fraternise with the fellow convert. The owner happened to be none other but John Kent, the author of the most dependable and unsentimental trout guidebooks to New Zealand. The Cruiser was his most recent acquisition, on its maiden voyage into the bush.

There they were, John and his long-time partner Patti Madsen, rigging up, about to start on their beat towards Lake Christabel. I'd never met them before but they cut unmistakably recognisable figures: John in his ageless and misshapen hat, which he must have got, already well-used, with his first-ever fly rod; Patti with her triathlete's physique and a mop of snow-white hair bristling above a visor cap, her fingernails painted carmine red, just as I remembered them from the guidebook pictures of trophy trout she held there.

We chatted briefly, about places which were in their guidebooks and about other, more secret ones which they vowed never to name and describe, and then they were off, stalking the high banks of the Blue Grey, one on either side, a picture of harmony in togetherness and contentment.

I knew nothing of their personal life, but the mind was quick to take a snapshot of this streamside happiness, filling in the blanks. What a perfect scenario for a fulfilling life: living and sharing the passion for trout, travelling, hiking and camping together, probing the mystery of the great fish. How many of us secretly yearn for this? How often are we disappointed when the 'significant other' does not share our passion?

Most men, it seems, consider fishing an escape from their wives or partners and the domestic life, a sacred time to be spent alone or only with the best of friends. But what if you could do what you love with the one you love most? How much better this could make the fishing, how much more fulfilling.

Of course, imposing the burden of such a dream on your loved

But what if you could do what you love with the one you love most? How much better this could make the fishing, how much more fulfilling.

one was a recipe for disaster, a trip-long divorce as no doubt many had found out for themselves. How many expensive fly rods, bought as Christmas presents for wives, gather dust at the backs of wardrobes? How many of those wives were getting bedsores on their behinds from hours spent waiting in the car?

What if there were better ways? Maybe the secret was not in what but in how? Because, if I really asked myself, it was now clear to me that if I could not do this with Ella I most likely would never do it at all. But maybe not all was lost. Maybe it wasn't too late. In any case, what did I have to lose that was not lost already? And so I sent Ella a text.

'How you doing?'

The answer came almost immediately.

'Still in damage control but ok. Breathing. You?'

'I'm by the river near Blenheim and . . . I miss you . . .'

After a long silence the phone chimed, and the message appeared.

'I miss you too.'

A surge of hope. I checked the time. It was just after 9 p.m. If I took the inland road, if I drove hard but still rested regularly, I could see her by the late morning.

I opened the back door and called in the dog.

'Maya! C'mon puppy-dog. We're going home.'

chapter 4

We sat on a rock overlooking another long and promising glide, and we ate our lunch and drank cold beer, and I thought that if there was some method of measuring the levels of happiness and joie de vivre in my blood the way cops test for alcohol I would certainly be well over the limit.

DEREK GRZELEWSKI

That late spring and early summer we got to fish a lot of still water at home. There wasn't much choice. Like ocean breakers crushing over a lonely rock, one westerly storm after another came in from the sea and swamped the island country, turning the rivers into dirty torrents on the windward side, creating more hellish gales down the lee slopes of the Alps. These waves were spaced two to four days apart so the rivers never fully cleared, before discolouring again and rising at alarming rates. Thomas Brunner would have related to it, I'm sure.

But within each storm cycle there was usually a day of calm, like a gap between the planetary breaths, and these we took with gratitude because, if you were into sight-fishing, they were the only times to make it happen. These were the days of stillness and crystalline beauty, with all the dust washed out of the air so that the world was crisp and fresh, and often touched with new snow which came on the tail end of the storms.

The trout too seemed to take advantage of these days, and along the edges of lakes they were plentiful and hungry, if a little wary of the attention they received from fly-fishers who could not go elsewhere. Still, there are miles of shorelines here — weed beds, and rocks, and edges of the drop-off — and if you chose your spots wisely, and avoided the obvious roadside access, the fishing was some of the best I had known. I spent one of those halcyon days with my friend Craig Smith, a Wanaka guide and — by necessity if not quite by choice — something of a stillwater expert.

A year earlier, his twin daughters were born on the opening day of the fishing season and from the hospital ward he sent out a group text which read: 'Two perfect females, 5½ and 6 lbs.' Replies congratulating such a stellar start to the season — good catch and a couple of keepers — poured back and some even went as far as to suggest he'd name the girls Rainbow and Brook.

Craig is the rarest kind of a fishing guide, always under-promising and over-delivering. He will walk your arse off looking for trout, not to impress but because this is how he likes to fish himself, and he creates opportunities with astonishing regularity. At the end of such walks he may leave you at the pool with a fish or two in sight and trot all the way to get the truck so that you wouldn't spend your fishing time walking back. Then, in the hut, he would cook the feast of a meal, get you merry on good whisky, dinner wine and après-fish stories by the fire, and when you were pleasantly woozy he would crash on a bunk next door as instantly as if flipping some internal switch. He'd be up before the first light, perky as a newborn and serving fresh espresso while you

He'd be up before the first light, perky as a newborn and serving fresh espresso while you were still massaging the sleep out of your eyes and the hangover of the epic yesterday.

were still massaging the sleep out of your eyes and the hangover of the epic yesterday.

With such aptitude and commitment, there is little wonder that, come fishing season, Craig is booked out, with all the spare time he has, and much that he doesn't, devoted solely to his family and the newly found delights of fatherhood. But disciplined man that he is, Craig still takes his days off and, lucky for me, I sometimes get to fish with him then.

That day at mid-morning, when the light was just high enough to start seeing fish, we had a quick scout near the boat ramp at the northern end of Lake Hawea. A slight breeze corrugated the water and it should have helped our shenanigans, but the trout there appeared uncommonly harassed. They milled about, visibly agitated and shying from anything we cast at them, often even before the line hit the water.

'Looks like everyone else has been trying here too,' Craig declared. 'Let's scoot across and find some fresh water.'

Next, we were ploughing a deep wake across the lake, heading for the eastern shore which is accessible only by boat or a long and tortuous 4x4 track. We saw the first fish even before the Stabicraft nudged into the sandy bank. Craig whipped out his rod, cast, hooked the fish and promptly lost it.

'That's more like it,' he turned to me with a wide grin. 'Let's go for a walk.'

The lake was glassing out now, with only moving skeins of opaqueness, like breaths of frost, marring its surface wherever the dying wind touched it. The sun was high, the sky cloudless and this made for perfect visibility. There were fish everywhere, moving sloth-like through the shallows, each one attended by the twin of

THE TROUT BOHEMIA

> '*They are not resting at all . . .*
> *they're ambushing bullies, lying still*
> *and camouflaged, until a bully*
> *swims within a striking range.*
> *Then you see them explode into*
> *action. Just watch.*'

its shadow, so crisp and defined you could see all of its fins. The shadows appeared bigger and sharper than their owners and it was easier to look for them first, then let the eyes travel up to find the fish that cast it, its elaborate camouflage suddenly useless, betrayed by the spotlighting effect of the sun.

Among the submerged boulder fields that made up the littoral zone of the lake the trout followed the contour of the shoreline, often less than a metre out. They moved with dignity and poise picking off nymphs with surgical precision. But wherever there were weed beds, every sandy patch of the bottom within them had a fish lying doggo, fins splayed out on the sand, unmoving like a statue. I had always taken such fish for ones who are resting and who, not feeding, would not be interested in a fly. But now Craig dispelled this falsity.

'They are not resting at all,' he said. 'They're ambushing bullies, lying still and camouflaged, until a bully swims within a striking range. Then you see them explode into action. Just watch.'

Sure enough, within moments there was a burst of sediments over one of the bare patches among weeds. It happened so fast we had to extrapolate that what we had just witnessed was a snake-like strike and a gulp. Even before the puff of sand dissipated the fish was already on the bottom and motionless again, back in its statue mode but poised for another attack.

Casting at such trout is a mistake that only perpetuates the illusion the fish is not feeding, Craig explained.

'Cast at it, or even near it, and you'll spook it for sure,' he said. What you need to do is to cast a bully imitation several metres

Stu Tripney's Pogo nymph

off to the side, then slowly, with short deliberate strips of the line, parade the fly into the trout's field of vision.

'In still water, trout are often triggered into attack mode by the little puffs of sediment the bully or the nymph make as they move along the sandy bottom,' Craig said. His bully was tadpole-sized, big-eyed, milky-white, semi translucent. And heavy. Each time it was lifted off the bottom it produced the desired puff of sand.

The exact imitation of the movement takes some practice and, early in the day, having not matched it correctly I had several fish ignoring my fly completely or swimming around it in agitation. You could just about read it in their body language — wide-eyed confusion: 'what the hell?' Some were interested but still not committing, coming back for another look, then another, before suddenly blurring off at speed into the safety of the deep water beyond the drop-off.

My casting was tolerable, but every now and then the muscle memory from a winter of using a heavy shooting-head line kicked in and my line came down like a falling tree, scattering fish in all directions.

'Yes,' Craig said, standing up after one such bungled ambush, 'it's definitely presentation, not detonation.'

It didn't matter. There were so many fish and so many

Moments later the ripples of splashes and wading subsided, and our world was again perfectly still. Just the two of us and the lake full of trout.

opportunities, we were often at a loss as to how to cast to one trout without scaring off several others, and so an occasional heavy-handed folly was a giggle not a regret. Maybe the days of foul dispiriting weather sharpened our appreciation because we both had a keen sense of just how perfect everything was. Whatever else was going on in our troubled world — the Arab Spring and more wars brewing, another banking crisis and other political machinations — all was well here and now.

There was not another boat on the lake, not a sound of a car anywhere. From our perspective Mount Aspiring showed its classic Matterhorn profile, sharp like a shark's tooth, and the reflections of other mountains in the water were so crisp it seemed the entire world was perfectly still and we and the trout were the only ones moving within it.

Past midday, we sat on a large rock overlooking a well-defined bay of fine trout terrain, ate our sandwiches while Craig brewed up coffee, barely taking his eyes off the water. When you're fishing with him even lunch is a form of sitting in ambush.

'You and Ella okay?' Craig asked. We had both seen each other through past misadventures of the heart.

'Touch and go,' I said. 'More go than touch, actually. Bit of a stalemate.'

'Who's the stale mate then?'

'Well, we both try our damndest, but sometimes it just seems too hard.'

'Often it is too hard. But you still have to do it.'

I shrugged. I didn't know again. After a combustive reunion it had only taken a few days for both of us to fall back into the old behaviour. Conflicts and hissy fits. Walkouts and loaded silences. Tears. All seemingly over nothing. Men from Mars, women from Venus? More like from different galaxies, light years apart.

'If you want to, you'll find a way,' Craig said, never stopping to scan the water. 'The question is not if you can but whether you want to.'

Just then, in the same instant, we both saw a fish cruising towards our lunch rock, moving with deliberate slowness as if dragging the burden of its large shadow.

'Jeez, that's a beauty,' Craig whispered. 'Get in there, mate, it's your turn.'

It wasn't, but I didn't argue. Over the rocks we fished nymphs, not bullies, and I had a tried and proven set-up on, supplemented at Craig's insistence with the tiniest of yarn indicators. A practical guy, he is always more concerned with results than undue purity. I laid out a cast on an anticipatory course with the fish, straightened the line and let it settle. Crouched on the rock, shoulder to shoulder, we watched the fish approach.

'Give it a twitch now,' Craig whispered, and I did. From where we knelt we could see the puff of sand the movement had stirred.

The fish turned and in delicious suspended animation we saw it come in, then up, rising to the surface, eyeing the yarn indicator, nosing it, poised for a take.

'Get outta here,' Craig cried in disbelief, 'he wants to take it for a dry.'

Just then the fish noticed the nymph, and its lithe body coiled and turned for it, dipping down. An instant later the indicator followed it under. I lifted the rod and the water erupted with a fighting fish.

The battle was swift and confined. I kept the fish splashing while Craig leapt in to net it. We did not want it to run and spook the rest of the bay. Not exhausted by the fight, the trout shot away in a blur of gold as I upturned the net. Moments later the ripples of splashes and wading subsided, and our world was again perfectly still. Just the two of us and the lake full of trout.

I did not want the day to end. The sun, though skimming the ridges now, was still spotlighting the trout so they could not hide from us and, with every passing hour, the landscape in its entirety — the land, air and the huge body of water — seemed to be entering into an ever-deeper state of breathless stillness. But Craig's mind was already home.

'Better head back,' he said, motioning towards the boat. 'The day is nearly done and I've got to feed the animals.'

THE TROUT BOHEMIA

An hour later I watched him crawl and wriggle through the kids' pen pretending to be a fish to screams of delight from the twins. I watched him bathe and feed them, and babble sweet gaga into their laughing faces, and he seemed even happier than he was on the water, perhaps because after a lifetime of outdoor adventures these were now the moments of magic and grace he craved more than anything else.

There was, of course, much I wasn't seeing: the sleep deprivation and chronic lack of time, health and financial concerns, forced compromises, and the inevitable conflicts these would bring into even the most harmonious family life.

It was all an adventure, alright. Just the scenery was different. At the back of my mind his earlier words kept echoing: 'The question is not if you can but whether you want to.'

It was a good question. Just what was the answer?

chapter 5

'Angling is extremely time consuming.

That's sort of the whole point of it.'

TOM MCGUANE, *THE LONGEST SILENCE*

By mid-November the tempests of spring began to abate and the still, sunny cloudless days we so longed for — the optimal conditions for sight-fishing — finally became more frequent. One early morning on just such a day I drove to fish the Mary Burn with a friend and fellow trout bohemian, Anthony, the blinding white pyramid of Mount Cook guiding us in like a beacon across the sea of brown and empty tussocks that make up the Mackenzie Country.

Ant is a passionate and perseverant angler, a former cop and now a voluntary Fish & Game ranger. He had only just returned from a twenty-month motorhome journey around New Zealand during which, with his partner of twenty-three years Liz, they unhurriedly moved from one trout hotspot to another, with Ant exploring plenty of lesser known rivers in-between as well. Liz did not fish, but she was as excited about motorhome living as a child would be about overnighting in a tree house. A dressmaker and a fashion designer, she had her fabrics and patterns in the bus, a sewing machine running off solar power, a guitar for rainy days, and stacks of books.

'We'd go into town and find a second-hand bookshop,' Ant said, 'and we'd sell all the books we'd read and stock up on new ones, like you'd stock up on food for a long trip into the bush, thirty to forty books at a time.'

This would see them through any bad weather, and when the weather was good Ant would leave Liz to her sewing and he'd fish along rivers which were all new to him, never casting a fly until he saw a trout. All this made for an extremely satisfying lifestyle but also for quite a shock when there finally came the time to return to settled life. Although they still lived in it, the bus was now tethered by its power cord to an old church they had bought to renovate into a home, and Ant was, well, more than a little antsy about not fishing as much as he had so happily grown accustomed to. I didn't need to ask him twice if he'd join me on this trip into the Mackenzie.

In spring and early summer, these brown and barren plains through which so many good trout rivers flow can be a very special place, if you get the conditions right. Wherever there is moisture in this sunburnt landscape, along roadside ditches, spring creeks and rivers, a profusion of lupins comes into flower, their many colours vibrant like smudges from a painter's palette, and Californian poppies brighten the grey glacial gravels with patches of orange.

The rivers here are like veins of life flowing through a desert, shaded with willows and poplars, and, right up to Christmas, dependably full of trout. Above them, the Arctic terns, which come to nest among the river gravels, snow-white but fast and agile like swifts, are a sure sign that a hatch is breaking out. You can often see them several pools away, working the riffles, swooping and diving to pick off mayflies alighting from the water. The birds' visual acuity is phenomenal. Many times, fishing a dry fly, I had one tern after another follow my artificial as I was false-casting it through the air. Each bird would examine the fly closely, flying alongside it at this whip-cracking speed, never once getting fooled by what it was. Only the younglings would occasionally pick the dry fly from the surface of the water, hold it with surgical precision in their tweezers-like bills and hover with it for a moment, before dropping the fly back, never once hooking themselves either.

I parked at the intersection of the highway and the creek and we geared up.

'First time "no waders" this season,' Ant said, folding his neoprene gravel guards over the top of his boots. After the cold of winter and spring, it was liberating to fish in shorts and boots again, to move light and fast and more *au naturel*, unburdened by the stiffness and rustle of the waterproofs. We had both come to wear waders now only when absolutely necessary. In trout hunting as we practise it, there is often a lot more walking than there is fishing, and waders, no matter how well-fitting and breathable, can bring about episodes of heat exhaustion, especially during the long end-of-the-day walk back to the truck.

There is a better way to access the part of the Mary Burn we wanted to fish, following the new and easy section of Te Araroa, the 'Long Pathway' — the trail that now runs the length of New Zealand — but we didn't know about it then and so we set off downstream and cross-country, keeping far enough away from the water not to disturb it. The going was hard and slow for the Mary Burn is effectively a spring creek gathering itself from seeps and trickles in the surrounding tussocks, and so the land around it is a swamp full of unseen holes and oily black water. We waded through lettuce-fields of watercress the way you'd walk though deep snow, but leaving twin trails of unexpectedly large pug marks. The still air was heavy with the honey fragrance of lupins, intoxicating like new mead, at times spiced with a sudden whiff of fresh wet mint.

At an obvious turnaround point, the bottom of a promising pool which emptied into a long stretch of nondescript water below, we stopped and started fishing back up. I sensed trouble as soon as we looked upstream, and the feeling only deepened with every perfect pool and run we stalked. I have only fished the Mary Burn once before, up from its confluence with the Tekapo. I remembered seeing and catching fish in most pools, and this I told Ant even before we set out. It would be unreasonable to expect similar fish densities this high up the creek, but still you'd expected to see something.

Mayflies fluttered about, but there were no visible rises on the water, and where the trees lined and overhung the banks the creek was in deep dappled shadow, the chiaroscuro contrast hard on the eyes and impenetrable. Where there were no trees the glare off the water was so intense the surface appeared metallic and opaque, likewise impossible to see through. As we walked up the creek, the excitement of being on new water, unknown and full of promise, began draining away. So often, we are quick to point out that fly-fishing and trout are but an excuse to be near rivers. But would you still walk a river knowing it had no trout in it? Never mind catching, we at least wanted to see something, a sign of life, a hint that the trout were here.

'Man, this is tough going,' Ant muttered, squinting into the glare. 'With this light, I can't see shit.'

His eyes are better than mine, more patient at least, and by now we had covered a good mile of the creek without a single cast, creeping up one promising pool after another, staring into the water as if trying to X-ray it. The day was still windless and sunny. Perfect but for the acute absence of visible salmonids.

The water looked perfect too. Although in places the creek was not much more than a couple of metres wide, it had deep undercuts, stable pools and well-defined riffles. Textbook feed lines below which you knew, from instinct and experience, there had to be trout, even if you could not see any. Below one such place, where a thin neat bubble line formed against a high and shaded bank, I gave in to the gnawing temptation and blindly cast my Elk Hair Caddis into it. A question to the stream. Anyone there?

The answer was instantaneous. The fly, sitting high in the water and twitched about by nervous current, did not travel more than two metres when there was a loud splash of the take and a moment later a trout leaped high into the air, a crescent of rainbow, glinting silver. Splash! Another jump.

'Wow, there are trout in here after all,' I heard Ant at my side say. 'But so much for sight-fishing.'

We got to see the fish well, netting it together, me holding the n-shaped rod high into the air so that the line would not foul on the edge of the undercut we stood on; Ant kneeling on it, reaching

CDC mayfly emerger

down deep to scoop the fish out. Even in the net the fish was lithe and feisty, splashing us with plumes of water as it fought the sudden confinement.

Freed from the net, the fish shot off downstream as if in a deliberate show of power and speed, a spirit that could be caught, even killed, but never subjugated. I watched it go and felt happy and alive. Some of that spirit, that irrepressible life force trout have, must travel up the fly line and into our own being as we fight a fish, but its intensity always seems magnified by the ritual of freeing the fish afterwards.

I false-cast the fly a few times to dry it, cleaned it with Dry Shake, then lobbed it again in the creek, a couple of metres higher. Another fish hit it, hard, just as the bristly straw-coloured

Another fish hit it, hard, just as the bristly straw-coloured deer hair touched the water. Another rainbow trout was arching through the air, leaping high, bouncing off the water as if it was a trampoline.

deer hair touched the water. Another rainbow trout was arching through the air, leaping high, bouncing off the water as if it was a trampoline.

'No kidding,' Ant made a surprised face. 'I'd better get my fly in the water too.'

He did: the entire length of the next feed line which looked just as good. But no fish came to take his fly, identical to mine. It was the same up the next run, and the one after that. Silently, I began to worry, especially that, giving Ant all the best water and willing him to catch a fish of his own, I hooked another couple of rainbows, fishing as it were, behind him. By then I was praying to all the deities I could think of that it wasn't one of those days when, fishing side by side, with similar abilities and exactly the same gear, one guy catches all the fish while his companion cannot touch a thing.

I needn't have worried. Ant is a fine fisherman, patient and unfazed. He was happy for me to catch all the fish I did, while not being unhappy about not catching any himself. A rare quality, wouldn't you agree?

I was releasing another one of my rainbows, which were all about the same size and fiery disposition, when I heard Ant shout an expletive monosyllable, and I saw his rod was bent hard, and then he was running up the side of the creek, scraping against bushes of briar rose and matagouri.

What a battle that was. His fish never jumped but it pulled hard, zigzagging up the creek, from one undercut to another, powering through the shallows with the snaking movement of its long glistening body, pushing bow waves up the pools. Ant followed the best he could, crossing and recrossing the creek while I ran along the bank, my net snagging repeatedly on the thorns of the bushes.

The underwater rocks were slippery with algae and so when crossing the creek Ant moved like an ice-skater, not daring to lift his feet up but sliding them along, feeling the contours of the bottom. And still the fish pulled upstream, gaining more line, as if it was heading for Mount Cook itself.

Then the fish stopped and as we both caught up with it, with Ant regaining all the line, we both saw why. My heart sunk. The line, still taut but now unmoving, was pointing into an impossible thicket. A part of an undercut bank, with the mother of a all gorse bushes on top of it, had collapsed into the creek, thorns and branches and all, and it was through this barbed tangle that Ant's trout had swum to seek refuge in the cavity behind it.

The fish was lost for sure, I thought. The line wasn't just snagged; it was woven into the gorse. Ant handed me his rod and I kept the tension on while he put his hand on the line and followed it down, disentangling it one thorn at a time. Next he was on his knees in the creek, up to his armpits in the thicket, working by feel alone, his face turned away from it, grimacing as the thorns raked and pierced his skin. And then he stood up laughing, stretching the kink out of his back, and in his hand, held by the tail, was a magnificent brown trout, burnished gold and intricately spotted, tired and subdued by being held upside down.

Ant unhooked it, and eased the fish in the water, holding it into the current, letting it breathe and recover. Then he let go of the tail and the fish held against the flow, nosing into the lee of Ant's boot as if it was a rock. For a long while we watched it, afraid to move and break the spell.

'I hope he's all right. Put up one hell of a scrap,' Ant said, and as he bent to check, the fish shot off upstream like a loosed arrow. We laughed and shook hands.

'Worth coming all this way for,' Ant said.

I felt exactly the same way.

We still had a mile of the creek ahead of us, the best part I thought, when, as if some invisible hand turned on an equally invisible fan, a downstream wind came down on us, the afternoon katabatic, straight from the mountains. The stream flows through open and exposed tussocks and, as the strength of the wind increased by the minute, it wasn't long before it started to wreck havoc with our casting. Even if the line, cast with a tight loop and a steeple backcast, went straight, the leader and tippet would get blown around and back.

'Put the fly on the water,' Ant offered as my casts landed on one bank then the other. 'Give the fish a chance to see it.'

But he could do no better himself and now we not only couldn't see but couldn't cast either.

'Call it a day?' Ant asked. There really wasn't much choice.

There is a good camp I always use when fishing in the Mackenzie, in the pines on the shore of the lake. It's sheltered from all winds and away from roads, with plenty of dead wood for campfires and an unrivalled view of Mount Cook National Park across the water, which is turquoise and thick with glacial silt.

We got set up there, and Ant read sprawled in a camp chair while, in a cast-iron camp oven, I cooked a venison stroganoff and served it with steamed quinoa and a Greek salad, and a bottle of heavy shiraz. Maya streaked about the woods and clearings, chasing rabbits. I once wondered why she never brought any home and concluded that perhaps, being fast and enthusiastic but heavyset and clumsy, and usually overshooting the tight corners, she couldn't quite catch them. Until one day, in an open field, I saw her cleanly run down and nab a rabbit, hold it for a while, then put it down gently the way a mother would put down a pup. She sat down next to it expectantly, a sprinter settled into a starting block, her eyes fixed on the terrified creature as if to say, 'Go on, let's have another round.' I guess it was her idea of catch and release.

After dinner we sat on our camp chairs by the fire on the edge of the beach. The wind had died now and across the lake the western faces of Mount Cook were aflame, twin daggers of warm light jabbing skywards from the deep-blue shadows that had already swallowed all other mountains.

'This is the life, eh?' Ant said, stretching in his chair, hands interlocked at the back of his neck. 'You know, Liz didn't want to stop travelling. If it weren't for the church project we would still be on the road.'

'How do you two do it?' I asked. 'I mean, get on so well for so long?' Living in a motorhome was like sharing the confines of an ocean yacht, and twenty months of that would have been an equivalent of a round-the-world sailing. It could make the best of friends fall out with each other.

'I guess the main thing is we never argue.'

'Never?'

'Well, nearly. I mean, there's not an argument that's worth having, is there? I learnt that as a cop. You can turn a most benign situation into a knife-fight by saying something stupid at a wrong time. You want to diffuse the conflict, not aggravate it.'

'So what d'you do?'

'It's simple: you see an argument brewing up, you walk away. Not storming off and slamming doors, but you walk away. So you don't get pulled into it. You defuse the conflict because the other person has no one to argue with. It's not nearly as satisfying to argue all on your own.'

'And then what?'

'When things have cooled off you come back. Offer a cup of tea. You're both reasonable again so any problems can be worked out.'

'That simple, huh?'

'It's never simple. But, in the end, what does it matter even if you win an argument? If you always need to be right you're just imposing your opinion on the other. That's not relating, that's tyranny isn't it?'

I did not answer. What Ant was saying seemed simple and obvious yet it was also surprisingly profound, a piece of the puzzle in the picture of human interactions that I should have got a long time ago but somehow missed until now. Or maybe it was always there, and I just never recognised it.

'You have your opinions, she has hers,' Ant went on. 'Both are fine. You don't have to agree, but you don't have to fight over it either. Just accept the differences and get on with the good things in life.'

He got up, stretched and broke into a chuckle.

'Women are complicated, man.' he said. 'Being with them is like fly-fishing. Sometimes it defies all logic and reason.'

He headed for the dome tent I put up for him and I heard him rustle about inside, his headtorch throwing theatrical shadows on to the blue fabric.

'Good night,' he said. 'It's gonna be another good day tomorrow.'

The daggers of light across the lake were gone now and I sat by the dying fire, digesting what I had just learnt, feeling a glimpse of clarity where in the past there had been confusion.

Why don't they teach this stuff at school? It should be on every curriculum, lesson one, page one: introduction to human relationships. We come into this world with no instruction manual for life and we bumble around snatching insights and gathering bits of understanding. There is no logic to it but there is grace, even if sometimes, like the fish on the Mary Burn, it may be impossible to see.

The following day we went even further up the Mary Burn, to where it flowed through Irishman Creek Station. The creek was smaller here, thin but beautifully structured with deep pools shaded by willows, and I wanted to visit it not only for the fishing but for the remarkable history of the place. It was here, in the now defunct sheds and workshops we could see from the creek, that certain events transpired and inventions blossomed, and they took the world by storm and forever changed the ways of river travel.

It all started around 1905.

'Do have a ride in my boat, Miss,' the little angel of a boy implored, innocent and eager to please, and how could the governess refuse such earnest a plea? Not yet seven years old, this youngest of the Hamiltons' four children had a thing for boats and water. He was always playing on the irrigation dam and the creek that fed it. At first, he used a galvanised wash tub with two bits of board for paddles, then progressed to a raft which the station's blacksmith made for him from five-gallon oil drums and bits of timber. Next came a canoe with an old sheet for a sail, and now this contraption of a boat which the boy had built himself.

She had to give him credit for ingenuity. The boat was cleverly made from bamboo rods and canvas, and so light little Billy could carry it all by himself. But this was also what made her nervous about it. The craft looked fragile and oh so unstable and she was a woman of portly stature. A small barge would seem a more appropriate vessel. The creek too was deep in places, especially the pool downstream of the homestead.

Still, the little imp would not relent.

'It's quite easy,' he went on, wading in to steady the craft. 'I'll hold the boat while you get in.'

The moment she stepped in and lowered her bulk into the canoe the governess knew it was a mistake. But too late. Billy had already pushed off the canoe downstream, towards that deep pool. The boat teetered as it ran out of momentum, then seeking new balance it upturned with a splash and the world of the governess instantly became wet. To-the-skin and through-all-skirts-and-petticoat kind of wet.

As she foundered, found the bottom and got up to her feet,

bedraggled and dripping, the little rascal was nowhere in sight, probably dancing a victory jig as he ran away to hide. Unbeknown to her, he would reappear by the creek later in the day, lured by the sight of an approaching visitor, the local minister.

'Do have a ride in my boat,' he offered sweetly.

'But I don't think it would bear me,' the reverend replied.

'The governess had a ride in it,' he reassured the man in cassock. 'It's quite easy. I'll hold it while you get in.'

The bamboo-and-canvas canoe may have been good for pranks that broke the monotony of station life — and indeed it notched up a few more unsuspecting victims — but secretly Billy Hamilton was unsatisfied with the design. It could handle the rapids on the nearby Opihi River, which was only navigable while in spate, but the problem was that, no matter how exciting, it was always a one-way trip. Downstream.

The current was too strong to paddle against and once the free ride was over there was the hard slog of carrying the boat back to the launching spot. In the wisdom of young years when anything is possible Billy reflected on the problem. What if he could . . .

Behind the blacksmith's workshop he found an old bicycle. He patched the flat tyres, made a wooden frame for the canoe and fitted it with bicycle wheels. In no time at all he had a boat trailer. Now what he needed was some horsepower to pull it. This came in the form of a reluctant brown retriever harnessed to the trailer with saddle straps cannibalised from the stables.

After much persuasion and a little training the beast would pull the trailer when ordered. The solution was workable but still cumbersome. What he really needed was a boat that could go upstream. Now, wouldn't that be a hoot?

He had no idea how that could possibly work, but by now he also knew that the world was full of wondrous challenges and that if he applied himself he could usually come up with a solution which worked. His mother had read somewhere that a child should not be encumbered with rigours of education until the age of seven, and thus until then she gave Billy a free range of the farm. His tutors were practical men of the land — farmhands, rabbiters, shepherds and blacksmiths. Toys too were scarce and in any case from the earliest days he preferred to make his own. As he grew older the toys became more sophisticated and refined.

In 1912, at the age of thirteen, and two years before the government's first hydro power station at Lake Coleridge, Billy Hamilton made a small dam across one of the gullies near the homestead, diverted some irrigation water into it, and built a flume which carried this water to a wheel turbine. This 'power station' generated about one horsepower of electricity, enough to light the house and to run a small lathe, a drill and an emery wheel his father had bought for him. Thus he came to have his first workshop, a favourite place to be and tinker.

Young Bill Hamilton just loved figuring things out, making sense of the world and the many ways it worked. Some of them still mystified him, though.

Take the ocean, for example. When they went to the coast near Timaru, his father told him about tides, how the water came and went, rose and fell twice every day and by as much as four to five metres. Yet when he filled a bottle with the very same water, thoughtfully making it only half full so that the water had room to move, it, well, didn't rise or fall at all. That just didn't make any sense, did it?

Fast-forward to 1923, when Bill Hamilton, freshly married to his soul-mate Peggy, struck out to make a pioneering life for themselves in the desolation and stark beauty of the Mackenzie Country. It was here, among the sepia-brown tussocks between lakes Pukaki and Tekapo, the land treeless and dry and rimmed by the skyline of the Alps, that he fully unleashed his creativity and problem-solving aptitude, allowing his unschooled engineering genius to flourish.

It was tough to carve a life and a living in this desert landscape. The soil was poor and windswept, and the winters harsh. The water race often froze solid, and life at Irishman Creek became a struggle to keep warm. In a letter home Peggy wrote:

> [We] are sitting [. . .] with our feet in the oven. I have never experienced anything like it. I spilt some boiling water on the stairs and when I came down two minutes later it was ice. Bread, milk and all foodstuffs are frozen and have to be thawed every morning. It is the worst for the children, and baby in particular. It is so hard to keep them warm in the morning.

Bill was literally living in his workshop, designing and building farm machinery, a sideline business that proved a saving grace for the family in the hard Depression years that followed. As the word about his inventions got out, contracts for earth-moving jobs began to flow in, first from local farmers, then from the government as well. Thus, when the economy slumped, when wool prices plummeted and stock was slaughtered because it could not be given away, Bill's machinery and skills came to be in such

Cyril and Jetske: 'In New Zealand we've found our promised land of fly-fishing, the trout bohemia.'

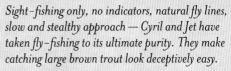

Sight-fishing only, no indicators, natural fly lines, slow and stealthy approach — Cyril and Jet have taken fly-fishing to its ultimate purity. They make catching large brown trout look deceptively easy.

The still-water perfection on Lake Hawea when the cruising trout seem the only moving feature in the landscape. Wanaka guide Craig Smith, who lives on the edge of the lake, surely knows how to pick such days.

The Mary Burn, against the backdrop of Mount Cook, is as scenic as it is exposed. The surface glare is intense and, unless the trout are rising, sight-fishing is a tough proposition.

Superb spring-creek brown trout, caught, landed and released, and never taken out of the water.

PJ and Lizelle, best buddies in life, business and on the river. With eyes like fish eagles and angling expertise to match they don't miss much of the trout action.

PJ says: 'I couldn't live in New Zealand. I would just fish, fish and fish and never get anything else done.'

Miles Rushmer demonstrates the perfect form of bow-and-arrow casting. The real-life applications are rarely as clean or as simple.

Five double-figure fish, one cast. Fancy your chances? Yours truly, against impossible odds.

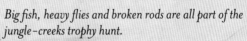

Big fish, heavy flies and broken rods are all part of the jungle-creeks trophy hunt.

The Tongariro River, fabled for its runs of winter rainbows, is equally good during the summer dry-fly season. Ten-pound tippets and ear plugs are essential: the fish are strong, like wild horses, and the song of cicadas can be deafening.

demand he had to hire a station manager so that he could fully
devote himself to the new venture.

He built the Hermitage aerodrome in Mount Cook village and
more airstrips soon followed: Gore, Haast, Kerikeri and Great
Barrier Island, then stopbanks in Karamea, roads in Spirits Bay,
a coal-stripping job in Mataura. Meanwhile, Bill continued with
his other inventions and designs. A shingle loader with a vibrating
screen. A 'travelling' water sprinkler. A haylift for stacking hay. An
air compressor. An air-conditioning unit for his daughter June
who suffered from hay fever. A machine for scraping, planing
and polishing the outdoor ice rink into mirror-like perfection.
The Irishman Creek workshop was now more a manufacturing
plant than a farm shed, and men who gravitated towards it, usually
retrained farm labourers, toiled over machines and prototypes
which the market snapped up as soon as they were ready. Among
themselves, quietly and reverently, the men referred to Bill
Hamilton as The Boss.

Alf Dick, a farmhand who became one of Bill's leading men,
recalled: 'The Boss was always quiet. He'd never growl at you, yet
we were in awe of him and took a lot of notice of what he said. If
you were doing a job and he saw you were going the wrong way
about it he'd never say more than "I'll think you'll find yourself in
trouble that way", and he was always right.'

Peggy wrote:

> In the evening he never relaxed by the fire, but worked hard and
> usually until a very late hour in the workshop or drawing office,
> and when at last he came in he would sit for hours absorbed in his
> drawings, working out some new scheme, oblivious to the time.
> On every shelf, edge or table I would find small scraps of paper,
> opened-up envelopes, anything that could be scribbled on with
> drawings of his ideas as they came to him. The evenings were
> always Bill's best time to work. [. . .] We never, or seldom, spent
> an evening together as a family. Even with visitors in the house he
> would be absent for most of the evening. All of us would be occupied
> each with his own particular hobby until sleep drove us all to bed.
> Bill was always last.

The projects the company undertook under Bill's leadership
remain major engineering feats even today. There was the
first ski rope tow up Coronet Peak, then the chair lifts and the
Queenstown gondola. There was the arched Kawarau Bridge and
the intake gates for many of the country's hydro schemes.

By the early 1950s, with his son Jon now at the helm of the company, Bill Hamilton began withdrawing himself from the business. Not to retire, you understand, just to retreat and tinker in the quietude of his Irishman Creek workshop again. He had an idea he wanted to pursue, one that harked back to the days of the bamboo-and-canvas canoe and the dog harnessed to pull it back upstream. The results of his labours would be what he is now universally recognised for around the world — the jetboat and the water-jet propulsion system.

It started innocently enough, with an ordinary outboard-driven boat, and an added aircraft propeller at the back to be used when the water became too shallow for the outboard. This attempt at turning a boat into a hovercraft was both comical and frustrating. The vessel made some headway up the Dobson River, but, as Peggy recounted, 'the efficiency was low, the noise and draught terrible and the spinning airscrew presented a constant danger of decapitation'.

After a few more futile attempts Bill turned his mind towards water-jet propulsion. The idea was not new. In 1661 two English inventors, Hayes and Toogood, toyed with it, and even as Captain Cook was navigating the world another two of his countrymen, Rumsey and Allen, designed a steam-driven jet unit which drew in water at the bow of a boat and ejected it at the stern.

In 1888 the first steam-powered jet lifeboat was commissioned in Britain, but it was not considered a success, and by 1900 the idea of water-jet propulsion was almost universally dismissed as 'inherently inefficient'. In every test conducted thus far the conventional prop-boat outperformed a water-jet, delivering more speed for less horsepower. Until Bill Hamilton took this on as his personal challenge.

George Davison, a marine engineer who became Bill's close associate, would later explain the principle of jet propulsion in a most graphic way: 'The reader will know the recoil of a rifle as the bullet speeds from the barrel. Has he ever felt the thrust when holding a powerful firehose? It is the reactionary force that is harnessed to propel the jet aircraft — and the Hamilton jetboat.'

Bill's first jetboat, named *Whio*, was a plywood 12-footer with a Ford engine powering a centrifugal pump via bevel gears. The pump sucked water through the grill in the boat's bottom and expelled it out the elbow nozzle. The jet's outlet was below the water level and the boat could be steered by pivoting the nozzle. But the steering was clumsy, the power transfer inefficient. After a test ride on the Waitaki, Peggy wrote: '[This] cockleshell of a boat had maximum speed of only 11 mph, which made the slightest ripple in the river seem a major rapid; but at least she was making headway against the river.'

More experiments on the Irishman Creek dam and its water race, and more tinkering in the workshop, brought about two conceptual breakthroughs. The first came in 1954 as an offhand suggestion from Alf Dick. What if, Alf proposed, the jet nozzle would be placed not under water but just above it? Apparently, being of slight built, Alf had learnt a thing or two about jet propulsion while handling the station's high-pressure fire hoses.

The Boss did not seem enthused about the idea, although clearly it must have percolated in his mind because next time Alf saw the prototype boat, only two weeks later, its thruster was above the waterline, and with instantly noticeable results. The speed was nearly doubled and the craft's response to steering was instantaneous.

The second improvement came in 1956 through the input from George Davison who simplified and streamlined the existing design. He took out the noisy bevel gear drive and changed it to a direct shaft. Then he did away with the centrifugal pump, replacing it with an axial-flow one, adding a second impeller for extra thrust.

Within a year of more trials and tweaks the boat was capable of doing 80 kph, travelling across water less than ten centimetres deep, and turning about, at full speed, within the space of its own length. This last manoeuvre, which today makes thousands of jetboat tourists squeal with adrenalin-induced glee, became known as the 'Hamilton turn'. Having overcome the problem of inherent inefficiency Bill himself took great delight in naming his boats along a fishy and distinctly anadromous theme which conjured up images of power and grace against fast currents. His subsequent models were called *Rainbow*, *Quinnat* and *Chinook*. The modern jetboat had arrived.

What followed was an era of exploration, first ascents and never-before-possible journeys, and again Bill Hamilton, by far the most experienced jetboat driver, led the way. A small group of enthusiasts formed around him and together they travelled the country notching up first ascents of rivers. They climbed the Clutha and the Buller and all of the east coast salmon rivers. Then they went up north where the jetboat caused an instant furore when Bill and Peggy ascended the 234-kilometre Whanganui River in just nine hours, four times faster than any boat ever before.

After this shakedown and learning period the jetboat and

its drivers were ready to tackle the world's most challenging rivers. The greatest show of all came in 1960, when the joint New Zealand–American expedition attempted to run the Grand Canyon section of the Colorado River upstream. It would have been fitting for Bill Hamilton to be there, but just a few months earlier he had broken his arm while boating the Matukituki River. He misjudged a turn coming too close to a rock and as he lifted his left hand to protect himself he wrenched it out of the elbow socket on impact. And so his son Jon and Guy Mannering went instead. They ran the river downstream first, over ten days laying caches of fuel and test-driving against all major rapids. After final tune-ups of the engines and jet units, they left Lake Mead and turned upstream to take on 539 kilometres of some of the most furious white water on the planet.

In 1869 John Wesley Powell made the first descent of the Colorado and portaged most of its major rapids. After completing the three-month journey he wrote: 'No man could take a boat into those rapids and survive.' Now, Jon Hamilton, Guy Mannering and their American companions set out not just to survive the rapids but to run against them, into the 50 kph current and mountains of white water.

Mannering wrote later:

> The trip up the river was the highlight of my life. I drove at the rapids sometimes as if in a dream, looking ahead at the ridiculous stepladder of muddy water; climbing up it incredulously not believing that any of this could really, or was, really happening. Vulcan Rapid (Lava Falls) was the greatest thing on the river. We used fifty gallons [189 litres] of gasoline to get the boats over the hill 400 yards long and rising about twenty feet in that distance. . . . Jon Hamilton drove each of the boats over the top and it was a great treat for us; son of the inventor drives first boat called Kiwi and three others over Vulcan . . . the first boats upstream ever.

It took Jon Hamilton two days to take four boats over the Vulcan Rapid, spending as much as half an hour to climb up individual standing waves. The passage earned the *Kiwi* an honorary place next to Wesley Powell's original oar-boat at the Smithsonian Institution museum in Washington, and the PR fallout from the expedition's success was such that a jetboat, whether as a tool or toy, became a new object of desire.

Little is known of Bill Hamilton's final years at Irishman Creek. What we do know is that to his last days he remained

> *This attitude probably makes him even more endearing because, in the culture of understatement, New Zealanders like their national heroes to 'knock the bastards off' and not brag about it.*

modest and unaffected by fame and fortune, dismissive of his own achievements, first to praise his co-workers and associates. The Boss was most remembered for his uncommon calm and composure, his practical jokes, the aura of pipe smoke and intense curiosity and concentration that surrounded him.

'I do not claim to have invented water jet propulsion,' he once said. 'The honour belongs to a gentleman named Archimedes, who lived some years ago.' This attitude probably makes him even more endearing because, in the culture of understatement, New Zealanders like their national heroes to 'knock the bastards off' and not brag about it. In this too, Bill Hamilton shall remain hard to best. He had asked, 'Would you like to come for a ride in my boat?' and the world has been saying yes ever since.

We did not see a single trout in the upper section of the Mary Burn nor did we catch one fishing blind. They just didn't seem to be there, and we concluded that perhaps the water was already too low and the fish had dropped downstream. All that was fine by us. We had an exciting stalk, full of prospects even if they never materialised, and Ant, a handyman himself, enjoyed my rant about Bill Hamilton.

By now the wind was picking up again, this time not the mountain katabatic but the harbinger of a weather front that was already pouring in from the west over the Main Divide. At the end of our beat the Mary Burn disappeared into a tunnel under the hydro canal — a two-level intersection of waterways — and from there we drove back along the ruler-straight bank of the canal. Most of the water was already ripped by the wind, but against one side there was a band of clarity in the lee of an escarpment. Ant's face was glued to the window.

'There's a fish! There's another one,' he pointed. 'A rise over there.'

I slowed down so he could spot his fish. The canals are full of them, trout and salmon — the latter being escapees from floating farms that are a big business here — and there is community of anglers who fish for them, living in motorhomes and caravan parked along the canal roads. Some spin but most fish bait — defrosted supermarket shrimp sunk deep to float just off the bottom — and their stubby rods are placed in holders and some have little tinkle bells at their tips. The anglers read and socialise while the fish more or less catch themselves. Over the years trout of world-record sizes have been taken this way. In 2009 alone, several fish in the 28 to 30-lb range were hauled out, including one 29.75 lbs and 34 inches (86.4 cm) in length caught by eighty-year-old John Meyer. In April 2002, American angler Mike Was pulled in a 37.41-lb rainbow here, still thought to be the world record.

I could hardly imagine Ant fishing this style, though, no matter how big the fish he could catch.

'There's one! Another just rose over there!' he enthused at the window, eyes scanning the water with the gaze of a predator. 'Man, I can't help myself. It's such a pleasure just to see them.'

This visual engagement, the thrill of possibility, seemed to totally satisfy him because at no point did he suggest that we actually stop and try to catch the fish, even though these trout were imminently catchable. By now he would have seen a good two dozen of them, and that after not seeing a single one on the Mary Burn.

As I slowed down to a crawl so that Ant could make the most of the remaining water, I thought of what my long-time river friend David Lloyd once told me about his fishing: 'What I find so endlessly fascinating in all this, what keeps me going for hours and days, is not that we catch fish, but that we *could* catch fish.'

chapter 6

'In some places and at odd times trout fishing can be easy in New Zealand, but typically and essentially it is more technically challenging and butt-kicking difficult than anywhere else in the world.'

CHARLES GAINES, *THE NEXT VALLEY OVER*

The best spring creek in the South Island of New Zealand, at least according to PJ, was this farm ditch meandering across Southland pastures, so overgrown with gorse, flax and manuka it would never occur to you to look for it unless you already knew it was there. And even then, the metres of thorny bankside hedge — what an ecologist would call a healthy and robust riparian strip but for which the rest of us would use other words, short and emphatic — would most likely deter you further as it enforced a long and muddy belly crawl with no guarantees of getting through.

There was no way to follow the creek, to walk its banks. PJ and Lizelle knew one entry point, the best one apparently, and once we wriggled through the hedge and into the water — into the cold, smooth, muscular flow — we stayed in it all day, waist-deep and more, sometimes tiptoeing through pools and troughs, pulling the tops of our chest waders up when the waterline threatened to overflow them. We had to return the same way, making sure we did not miss the exit point. Although the two of them had fished the creek for years and knew it well, PJ still marked the exit with a strip of coloured plastic. Coming down, I realised, we'd never find the way out without the marker.

At times the hedge banks met overhead and we waded through the tunnel, ducking under branches, threading our fly rods through the tangle. It was hard to spot fish in there because of the deep shadows, but in-between the tunnels there were large open weed beds, in full sun and with the hedge providing good backdrop. The waterweeds were in flower and the tiny white blossom sparkled and shimmered through the surface like snowflakes. Holding in among them, on the edges of weeds, in depressions and sometimes over clear patches of golden sand, were some of the hardest brown trout I've ever fished for.

For me, it was a grand surprise to be here at all. We were supposed to fish the upper Eglinton River, which I love, but early that morning in their truck, as they munched on organic venison pies and sipped takeout coffees that would keep them going all day, PJ and Lizelle broke into an animated discussion in their native Afrikaans. In turns they looked at the sky then talked some more. I could not understand a word but sensed that something weighty was being decided.

The day was as good as they come in fly-fishing: windless and without a cloud, promising to warm up to some good terrestrial action. We could have gone anywhere and Eglinton seemed to me an especially good choice.

Their debate over, PJ turned to me and said: 'Change of plans.

THE TROUT BOHEMIA

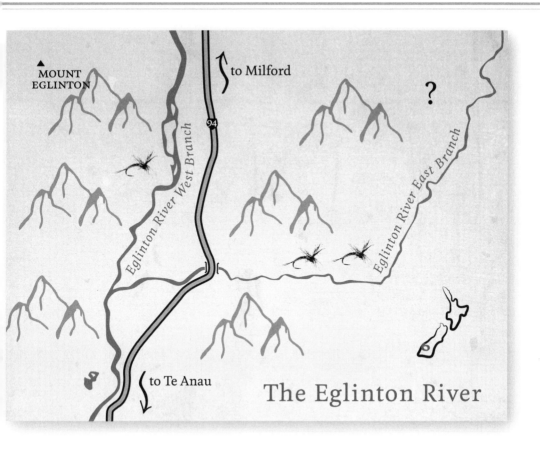

MOUNT EGLINTON

to Milford

94

?

Eglinton River West Branch

Eglinton River East Branch

to Te Anau

The Eglinton River

It's a very special day today. We'll take you to our most secret creek.'

'We'll have to blindfold you, though,' Lizelle said, handing me her camo Buff, 'and swear you to secrecy on the fear of feeding you naked to the hyenas.'

'Ah, and please hand in your iPhone and any other GPS devices you may have on you,' PJ said.

'You're not serious?'

''Course not,' Lizelle winked and put the Buff around the base of her moleskin sunhat. 'But go and get another one or two of these delicious pies. It's a long way and a big day out.'

On that long drive down we talked.

Eighteen years ago, PJ was a hot-shot lawyer in Pretoria and already mad about his fly-fishing. In his spare time, he took it upon himself to publish a small magazine — more a newsletter those days — for the South African fly-fishing community.

His vision was that the magazine's content should be 'by fly-fishers for fly-fishers', and the idea was so well received that within a few years and, now renamed *The Complete Fly Fisherman*, the magazine had grown into a full-time family business. Since then, with PJ as a discerning editor and publisher, and Lizelle in charge of its visual identity and advertising, the TCFF came to be regarded as one of the best such publications in the whole of Africa.

A month before they came to New Zealand this time, PJ and Lizelle put out the commemorative 200th issue of their magazine to which I'd been a contributor for a few years. We'd become good pen pals over the years, and so it felt we knew each other well, even if we'd only met in person for the first time the night before.

As owners of such a prestigious publication, PJ and Lizelle have been fly-fishing all over the world, both salt and fresh water. The best lodges, all the dream destinations, most of the fish species. But for the best in trout fishing they've always been coming to New Zealand and every year this has been their time out, special and sacred and something to look forward to, away from the business and its deadlines. A month to rest and recharge with — as one statement T-shirt put it — 'No cellphone, no email, no problem'. Their approach and style was not as bohemian as that of Cyril and Jet and far more comfortable, but the passion and skills were just as keen.

The oddest thing is Lizelle does not fish at all. She walks the rivers with her husband, wading stick in hand, waterproof camera bag on her chest, taking an uncommon delight in spotting the fish for him, and her eyes are as sharp and quick as those of a fish eagle.

'She's the only person I ever let walk in front of me on the river,' PJ said proudly. 'Between us, we don't miss much.'

Indeed. Even if the fish were in hiding. The previous day they did fish a section of the Eglinton and found that the river was scoured by floods, with huge trees lying everywhere. The beat was devoid of fish, which must have been washed back into the lake by the cataclysmic deluge. But, having considered that, and the question of 'where else the fish could have gone', in a sheltered side braid they found nine good trout and caught them all, which for Eglinton is exceptionally good going.

'Fly-fishing is a thinking man's pursuit,' PJ said, 'because right up to the moment of hooking the fish, which may take minutes, or all day, or may not happen at all, you're not fishing, you're thinking: where to go, how to approach a fish, what fly to use and so on. You observe and learn from what you see; you figure out strategies and eliminate those that don't work. All this engages your creative problem-solving mind, in a beautiful environment.

'Then you see people who just flog the water, without being present in what they're doing, just hoping that, if they do it long

'There are three kinds of anglers, three kinds of people, really: those who make things happen, those who watch it happen, and those who ask what happened?'

enough, they'd get lucky and something will happen. They don't observe, don't draw conclusions. You come back hours later and they're still in the same place, doing the same thing, hoping against hope.'

He laughed.

'There are three kinds of anglers, three kinds of people, really: those who make things happen, those who watch it happen, and those who ask what happened?'

From the start, however, making things happen on the secret creek was never going to be easy. PJ and Lizelle had walked the same section two weeks earlier (they didn't dare to come more often) and they saw maybe thirty fish, active and eager, and PJ caught a good number of them. This time we weren't seeing a lot of fish and some of those we did see held in the current with their heads and bodies buried in the weeds, only their tails visible. Others were dour and disinterested and some spooked even before we had a chance to cast. PJ's face grew troubled.

'This is not normal. The water looks fished, very recently, like yesterday,' he said, and we waded on, the two of them abreast and doing all the spotting, me bringing up the rear and looking over their shoulders as the creek was too narrow and delicate for any other approach.

'Ah, there's one,' Lizelle said, pointing out the fish with the practised slowness of a hunter. 'Left bank. Ten metres up. Just down from that overhanging flax branch.'

It was my turn and I cast: a fair and accurate effort. The fly went over the flax branch and the tippet wrapped itself around it once, only two inches or so but enough. As I pulled on the line to free it the leathery branch trembled and the fish shot off for the cover of weeds.

Over the next fish PJ put several immaculate casts, each time a different CDC fly drifting right over the trout's nose, without drag and on the finest of tippets. He was a superb angler, I thought, one of the best I'd ever seen in action. Yet the fish refused every one of his offerings and you could almost read the disdain in how it turned away from them. But, then, the fish was also ignoring natural mayflies floating by, never a good sign.

'Unbelievable,' PJ muttered. 'Usually, the fish here are not that selective.'

He puzzled over the contents of his fly box and his face lit up.

'Ah, perhaps we're fishing a little *ex abundanti cautela.*'

'Ex what?' I asked.

'With excessive caution. Or, in my liberal translation: "If you act like an asshole expect to be treated like one." Let's try something bolder, with a little more *je ne sais quoi.* A secret weapon.'

He put on another fly. I didn't quite see what he'd chosen, only that it was big and black as it floated down towards the trout.

'Would you look at that!' I heard myself laugh.

The reluctant fish did not examine the fly with an upturned nose as before. It shot a good metre upstream, making sure the fly would not get away, and it took it with the sound of a wet slap.

PJ struck and winced.

'I was afraid this would happen,' he said.

They landed the fish together, Lizelle netting it with an easy scoop.

'What was the fly then?' I asked.

'Ehh, I'd call it a Bluebottle Emerger.'

'You mean a maggot?'

PJ winced again.

'Such unfortunate names for the lowly flies, aren't they? Kind of compounds our distaste for them. You know, I'd rather catch trout, especially in creeks like this, on the noble and beautifully tied classic dry flies, but the fish would much rather eat this . . . this . . .'

He shook his head, unwilling to pronounce the word.

What the fish took was an imitation of a most foul creature, the bane of hunters and one major reason why the insecticide industry is a thriving business — the blowfly.

'Trout may refuse everything else, but they see one of these and they just can't help themselves,' PJ said. 'It might be the blue metallic iridescence in the underbelly of the fly that triggers the attack but, you can be sure, when all else fails, put on the . . . the . . . The Fly and more often than not it'll work.'

Sure enough, the next two fish were the repeat of the first one.

PJ rolled his eyes.

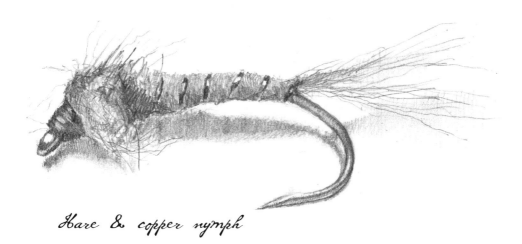

Hare & copper nymph

'This creek should be designated *Blowfly Only*.'

He could jest and mock the lowly blowfly. All three fish were his, beautifully conditioned, expertly caught. I would not have minded any of them, no matter what fly they took. But things were not going well for me. Next to PJ, with his precision, his light but confident touch and uncommon finesse I felt clumsy and graceless.

My gear was heavy too. PJ was fishing with his #4, me with a standard #6, and casting with a #6 on such delicate water was like shooting rabbits with a .270. It could be done, but it made a mess of things and wasn't at all satisfactory. Be it the gear or the pressure to perform in the presence of such expertise, all I'd accumulated so far was a string of unlucky mishaps, never big but enough to bungle the few opportunities that presented themselves. I hooked the only tuft of weed protruding next to the fish and spooked the trout. Once I put the cast down too hard, to the same effect; on another I just could not get a fly under an overhang where the fish was feeding. The sun was well past its zenith, we were coming to the end of fishable water and I still didn't have a single hook-up.

'That explains everything, why we're seeing so few fish and why they're so shy,' PJ said.

He pointed to a wide trail ripped through the bed of lettuce-like weeds.

'You don't have hippos in this country. Only a man would leave a spoor like this. Someone's fished this creek yesterday, or the day before. Such delicate water cannot take the pressure of more than one angling party a week.'

We went around the lettuce bed and up ahead the creek split in two and both branches disappeared under the thicket. This was the end of our fishing. Well, almost.

'My God. Look at that, would you?' Lizelle said, nodding to the split.

PJ whistled and said, 'Good heavens'.

The bigger of the two branches funnelled out from under the hedge and into a pool with a golden sandy bottom. On that bottom, and nosing into the narrows, sat an enormous fish, black like a cut-out silhouette against the brightness of the sand.

'Look at his pectoral fins,' PJ said. 'They stick out like wings of an aeroplane.'

I swallowed hard. My turn. Last chance of the day. And the biggest fish we'd seen so far.

Earlier I had put on Stu Tripney's bluebottle blowfly, tied Klinkhammer style, with a metallic blue underbelly and a hi-vis parachute post. Problem was there was nowhere to put the cast. The fish nosed right into the bottleneck of the current and right above it was where the hedge started. No amount of precision would place the fly where the fish could see it, without spooking the trout first.

PJ and Lizelle were off to the left, with a perfect view of the proceedings, giving me all the space I needed. But it was hopeless really because where the fish was he was pretty much untouchable.

'This is a big fish,' Lizelle said, as if I needed more pressure.

'He's huge,' PJ echoed. 'If you hook him, I hope you have a tippet of steel. Anything could happen here.'

I checked and rechecked my knots. They were solid, but I still could not see a way to cast to the fish and PJ understood my consternation.

'Don't cast at him, you'll only spook 'im that way,' he said, his voice now calm and comforting. 'Cast a couple of feet to the side, and make him come up for it. In this water he'll see everything, even if the fly lands behind him.'

Still I hesitated and for a long while we stood there, watching the fish, its feeding no more than a languid sway in the current.

Maybe I had notched enough strokes of bad luck that day, those micro-mishaps that kept me fishless, or maybe it was my turn for a touch of divine intervention. But just as I was about to cast, dubious about the prospects and with no room for error, the great fish saw something way off to the side and went for it, moving a couple of metres to the right from his position and for a second or two facing away from the funnel of current from which it fed. I used the moment of his absence and I cast, placing the fly right into the narrows just as the fish was looking away.

When he turned back he saw the fly, naturally coming down out of the narrows and, like all of PJ's fish earlier, he did not wait for it. He charged.

Before my fateful cast, I had silently recited to myself the astronaut's prayer. Attributed to Alan Shepard, the second person in space, and often repeated by aviators just before they make a landing, the prayer goes: 'Dear Lord, please don't let me fuck up.' So far, it seemed, my prayer was being answered. Everything now was happening as if in slow motion.

Over my shoulder I heard Lizelle's motordrive whirl like an old-fashioned movie camera. I lifted the rod and the line ripped an arrowhead wake of fine spray from the rod tip all the way to the fish. There was something akin to an underwater explosion where the trout had been, and I heard PJ yell: 'Ya man, you got 'im, man. You got 'im. You got 'im!'

In his excitement he had slipped into Afrikaans.

Earlier, PJ had explained to me his novel technique for landing trout. Instead of the rodeo approach of holding the fish up, keeping it flapping and not letting it fully engage its fins against the water, he would hold his rod down, pointing it at the fish, keeping the line lightly taut. Then, very gently, PJ would pull the fish towards himself, either reeling the line in or walking backwards. The fish usually did not fight at all.

'If you lift the rod and horse the fish it's only natural it will resist and fight back. It'll jump and run for cover and try to tangle you up. If you don't fight it, the fish doesn't fight you or suspect anything is wrong, so you can bring it in quietly before it knows what happened.'

When the fish did realise what was happening it was usually too late, the water too shallow, the line short, the landing net approaching.

'The only disadvantage of this technique is that when you net the fish it is still very green, full of unspent energy, so unhooking and photographing can be problematic.'

I saw him use this technique several times, and it worked well, but this was neither the place nor time for such counter-intuitive experiments. I kept my big fish splashing, confusing its sense of directions by sword-fighting the rod left and right, reeling in as fast as I could. It was a quick and forceful combat. In a place so full of potential snags I did not dare let the fish go anywhere.

We closed in on the splashing trout and netted him. We estimated it was pushing six pounds but none of us carried scales.

'My God, he's the best fish I've seen in this creek for a long time,' PJ marvelled. 'Look at him! Look at the hump and the kype, the fierce glint in its eyes. It's so good to see. He's not some old fish living out his days. He's young, fat and strong, and he'll grow bigger still.'

I let the fish go and he sunk to the bottom and held there, nosing into the weeds. We stood motionless watching him, soaking in the moment.

'What did he take?' PJ asked when the fish was gone.

'A bluebottle emerger,' I said.

'I feared this much. This creek is abuzz with mayflies, hatching, laying eggs, fluttering about. You seine the water, study the food profile to match it, you make an educated decision and . . . put on a blowfly.'

We laughed. It was time to wade back.

On the way down, perhaps buoyed by the fact that despite tough fishing the day was turning out better than he thought it would, PJ got talkative. He was worried about the creek, and about the laissez-faire attitude of New Zealanders towards treasures such as this.

'My grandfather had a farm where we had to shoot lions to protect stock. Hunting was a big thing for me then, but now I wouldn't shoot a lion, or any other animal. It's fly-fishing that made me into a conservationist. Once you sample the pleasures of being in places where trout live, once you engage with its habitat, you realise how precious it is and you want to protect it at all costs.'

He paused, considering something.

'If this creek was in our country, it would be totally taken care of. It would have full-time gamekeepers looking after it, insect profiles studied, the access would be strictly controlled. One party would be allowed to fish it once a week and it would cost a fortune, and you'd have to book it months in advance. That's how special this place is!'

They were wading down the creek side by side, arms wrapped around each other's shoulders, best mates doing what they love, in their favourite place in the world.

'We've been coming here for thirteen years, and we've only just scratched the surface of things,' PJ said. 'There are some three hundred rivers in the South Island alone. For wild trout, New Zealand is a phenomenal place. There is nowhere better.'

He shook his head and laughed.

'I couldn't live in this country. I'd just fish, fish and fish every day. I'd never get anything else done.'

Was it why my own To-Do lists were never getting any shorter?

Back at the truck, after we'd taken off the plastic trail marker and

'There are some three hundred rivers in the South Island alone. For wild trout, New Zealand is a phenomenal place. There is nowhere better.'

fought our way through the hedge again, PJ pulled out three chairs, a chilly bin for a table, and a well-iced bottle of Moët & Chandon.

'As I said,' he turned to me, 'today is a very special day in the Jacobs' household. It's our sixteenth wedding anniversary.'

They met at the Nooitgedacht Trout Lodge, a luxury retreat on the Spekboom River three hours east of Jo'burg. PJ was fishing and Lizelle was on a girlie weekend getaway with her friends. They got talking at the dinner table. She liked his stories, intelligent and well told, and he thought she was a real babe, and a hell of good photographer. They left it at that, but not for long.

Seven years later, in the same lodge, he proposed to her, dropping to his knee and unstopping a bottle of Moët. He says she accepted and swooned into his arms, but Lizelle's version differs slightly. Apparently, she was drunk and muttered an incoherent reply, and he interpreted it as a yes; since he was a lawyer, he felt her words were legally binding. Couldn't get out of it if she tried.

They laughed and embraced and, on the chilly bin by the secret creek, PJ refilled the champagne glasses.

'Some of my best river friends can't get their heads around the fact that Lizelle always comes with me on all fishing trips,' PJ said. 'They think these trips are supposed to be gentlemen-only kinds of outings, away from home, away from their women. And I tell them: "I love you all like brothers but I'd always — always — rather fish with my wife than with any of you." Most of them don't get it.'

I did get it.

'PJ, you're the luckiest bastard I've ever met,' I said.

'I am,' he grinned. 'And I know it.'

Lizelle asked about my own affairs and I told them. I held nothing back, reasoning that, if anyone could offer advice or help it would clearly be someone like them. After all, they were living the very thing I aspired to.

I told them how, despite all Ella and I seemed to have going for us, there were so many 'irreconcilable differences', the smallest issues always seemed to explode into unsolvable quandaries. Everything was a problem: the time together and the time apart, especially the time apart.

Lizelle listened and frowned.

'If you have to claim your time, defend and justify it, if you feel guilty doing what you love because you think you should be back home with her, the whole thing will never work or last,' she said.

It was a hard thing to hear.

'You have to stay true to yourself, both of you, true to who you are and what's important for you,' she went on. 'Then it's really simple: you're either compatible or you're not. Have you tried to talk about it?'

We have, I said, but it was no good. It only led to more conflict over things which, a few days later, we could not even remember.

'When I was practising law I dealt with a lot of divorce cases,' PJ said. 'If there was one thing I learnt from all that it's that the secret to all relationships is good communication. Without that you have nothing. No basis or way to resolve any issues and so they accumulate until they're too much to handle, and it all falls apart.'

Clearly, they didn't have this problem. Or any other problems, it seemed. Over the next few days we fished other rivers and we found plenty of fish, and caught many of them. I was inspired by PJ's fishing finesse, a whole new level of it, and resolved to refine my own ways: polish up my casting, get lighter gear and learn how to use it. What struck me most, however, was the rarest kind of harmony between these two. Whatever they did, they did together, and in that they were at the top of their game: in fly-fishing, in business, in love as in life.

Some guys have all the luck, eh? Or maybe they are just better at helping it to happen.

chapter 7

'A trout is a moment of beauty known only
to those who seek it.'

ARNOLD GINGRICH

After *The Trout Diaries* was published a good number of readers took time to write to me. This was not really fan mail, more a nod of acknowledgement that they understood what I had attempted to convey. That they too fished for similar reasons even if they have not put them into words, and that there was among us a spark of recognition that we were of the same tribe and, most likely, if we ever met, we would get on well on a river. Some wrote at length about their own experiences: the seductive intensity of sight-fishing, how the seasons changed on their home rivers and how at different times they went to them to seek solace, to celebrate, or just to be in their quiet dependable company.

Others wrote how fly-fishing had helped them through illnesses, broken marriages and other calamities, and how it too delightfully dominated their lives, from the colour of clothes they now wore and the kind of car they drove, to how they saw the rest of the world and their place within it. Of all these emails and letters none had touched me more than the story of Richard and his giant fish.

Richard was born in Cleveland, Ohio. He came to New Zealand on fly-fishing holidays, fell in love with the place, and two years later came back to stay for good. That was some twenty years ago and now he had a small business in a small town in the southern part of the North Island, a steady and loyal clientele and no desire for growth and expansion. This arrangement allowed him plenty of spare time, much of which he spent in pursuit of trout. Years ago he had fallen under the spell of Roderick Haig-Brown's idea 'to know a river' and he chose his home river — medium-sized and not particularly famous — and got to know it about as well as you could.

The river was good to him and he liked to see it change through the seasons, from the spring budding of new leaves to their spiralling fall into the water in autumn. 'Over the years I've probably fished every day of the season on this river,' he said, 'and I've rarely seen another angler.' The river trail was kept open mainly by his own frequent passages and he liked to walk it in the off-season too, to check on the river and to watch the fish, and to dream and anticipate what the new season would bring.

On his river, there was a deep pool choked with willows and brambles, impossible to fish or even to look into. Richard had often walked past it but always sidled around the thicket, and if he spared it a thought it was usually a curse. He had caught a few good fish upstream of the choke but lost every single one of them once they ran down and into the logjam, through the curtain of willow branches trailing in the current.

Then one day, returning along the trail, he saw a distinct flash of silver in the small space where horizontal willow logs overhung the river. A fish? If it was a fish it was big! A salmon? That was unlikely. So what on earth was it?

He was intrigued. There was no way through the thicket, but next time he brought hand clippers and garden gloves, and he cut a thin trail, pulling the tangled branches out like strands of barbed wire. Past the brambles, there was an easier but still tight wriggle through the willows, with their low limbs bristling with vertical shoots, dense as a hedge. With more judicious pruning, crawling and squeezing through, he finally got his first glimpse of the pool.

The water was dark and slow-moving, backed up against a natural dam of sunken logs, and at first he could not see anything in its depths. But as he gazed into it and his eyes adjusted to the half-light, he realised that what he first took for a long fat branch parallel to one of the logs was not a branch at all. As he looked harder, the outline of the fish appeared in his vision like a shape hidden in one of the 3D Magic Eye pictures. He could only see the head, just past the gills. The rest of the fish was in the gloom, under the logs.

He saw the profile of a huge upper jaw, and where the line of the nose should have been there was a deep groove that ran towards what looked like nostrils and, there, the formidable hook of the lower jaw — the kype — came up to fit in-between them.

This fish was old, Richard thought. Very old. There was something ancient, almost reptilian about it, and it reminded him of crocodiles he saw in northern Australia, lying in wait, still but coiled for a strike, oblivious to the passage of time. The giant fish had obviously known anglers. There was a rusty old spinner hanging from the corner of its mouth, two barbs of the treble hook fast in the cartilage of the lower lip, the third one protruding out like a bad tooth, a tiny red tag hidden behind the discoloured silver spoon. The movement of the jaws was almost imperceptible as the fish took in water to breathe.

For a long time Richard stood there, moulded to the trunk of the willow, watching the giant trout. Then, when his back grew achy and stiff, he withdrew with infinite slowness, careful not to alert the fish.

He could not sleep that night. He had caught some big fish in his days. In the headwaters of the Rangitikei and the Mohaka, in the Tongariro, in Fiordland and north-west Nelson but, at least judging from the size of the head, he had never even seen a fish this large. And it had lived, would you believe it, and who knew for how long, in an unseen hole on his home river which he had walked so many times.

Over the weeks that followed Richard began visiting the fish, not to catch it but to watch. He had cleared a path to the pool, minimal and blocked at the entrance with a vicious-looking bramble, and he would forgo his usual fishing, and the clockwork hatches that were happening right now, to lie on his belly on a willow limb above the pool and feast his eyes on the wonder below.

The river here turned a dogleg and, in the corner cutting deep into the bank and framed by the logjams, the current formed an eddy with a feed line spiralling in on itself so that all the great fish had to do was to lie in it and open its jaws, its mouth at the centre of the endless vortex of food.

The feed line was strong and well defined, but it did not froth or bubble, and so when the light was good Richard could see individual insects floating within it: large mayflies and skittering caddises, bumbling beetles and waterlogged hoppers. The fish swayed in the current with the efficiency befitting its old age and the takes were barely visible twitches of its great jaws, though some were hard and loud, and these sent Richard's heart racing.

Days and weeks had passed and by now Richard was even dreaming about the fish in his sleep. These were always lucid full-colour scenarios in which he could see his big and bristly dry fly approaching the fish, almost reaching its fluted nose, and the trout noticing it and swinging towards it, and then he would always wake up, bolt upright, and curse himself for not staying with the dream for just a moment longer.

But maybe it was better that way. Despite the dreams he never actually thought he would even try to catch the fish. It was an impossible proposition. There was no way to cast, and what if he managed to hook it? The fish would sure wrap him around the underwater logs and snap off any tippet. Best keep it as a dream only, he thought, a delicious possibility. The reality could be a crushing anticlimax.

Still, as he lay there on the log, wearing his full-camo bow-hunting gear, watching the fish from such intimate distance, a desire to engage with it began to grow within him, slowly but inexorably, a tiny spark at first, then a flame, then an all-consuming wildfire.

Maybe it wasn't so impossible after all. With some more pruning perhaps he could get the fly on the water where the fish could see it. And if it broke him off? Well, it wasn't much harm in that and he would have at least engaged with it. And there was the matter of

Once the thought took hold of his mind it became a gnawing obsession and Richard had to discipline himself not to rush his quest.

that old spinner too. Richard was sure it bothered the fish. Several times he had seen it take an angry swipe at it with its jaw the way a dog may snap at an annoying insect. If he caught the fish, and if, by some miracle, he managed to land it, he could remove that treble hook, free the fish from its disfigurement.

Once the thought took hold of his mind it became a gnawing obsession and Richard had to discipline himself not to rush his quest. With such an old and wise brute he'd most likely get only one chance and there were many things to consider: the right fly, size of the tippet, time of day, and what happened if he hooked the fish.

He had an old Tongariro rod and he made it into a half-length sawn-off, joining the tip and the butt so that he could work it in the confines of the thicket. It was ugly but felt strong and he practised casting with it; well, if you could call it that. It was more an off-the-water flick, and the tip worked, sort of, though the accuracy was always going to be doubtful.

From his recurring dreams he already knew what fly he had to use — a large and buoyant Elk Hair Caddis — and for time of day he chose dawn. This way he could get into the position while it was still dark and the half-light would help disguise the heavy tippet.

One day, watching the fish again, he identified all the branches which could be problematic. He returned on a stormy night, and as the trees swayed and rustled, with his foldable bush saw he cut off the offending branches, one by one, making it all look natural, as if they just snapped in the wind.

A couple of months had passed since he first saw the fish. He was now comfortable with the idea of trying to catch it but still somewhat reluctant, postponing the day with the meekest of excuses. Too overcast. Too windy. Not windy enough. More work needed on the new joint in the rod.

THE TROUT BOHEMIA

He realised that at the core of his reluctance was a deep fear. Not of goofing up his attempt, although that too gave him a heart flutter every time he thought about it. No, he was more concerned about the fish. Clearly, it must have lived there undisturbed for years. What if it spooked out of the pool and never came back? Where would it go? There was not another hole on the entire river that could be a home to a fish of this size. And still the dreams continued, repetitive and regular, and he could not make himself stay in them to see what happened. He would give it just one go, he promised himself. He had to try, but if it didn't work out he would not persevere. He would let the fish be, let the path overgrow again. But he had to try. Just once.

When the day came he rose before dawn. He had barely slept so the dream did not come back. No way could he eat anything and the coffee left an acidic taste in this mouth. Was it the coffee or the fear? He wasn't sure.

In the darkness he found his way to the pool, then with the slowness of a sloth he inched his way on to the limb of the willow tree that overhung it, the sawn-off rod at his side. He reached the position from where he hoped to make his one cast and waited for the light.

The day came slowly, filtering through the willows and gathering in strength as Richard lay on his stomach, feet hooked around branches for balance. It wasn't long before he started feeling stiff and uncomfortable, the studs and knots of the tree digging into his flesh and ribs, but he endured quietly, and waited in stillness as a hunter must wait. An hour passed, then another. The fish did not appear. When he could wait no longer, Richard eased himself back down from the tree, wincing at the aches and pains, then stretching and shaking himself loose once he was out of sight of the pool, bringing circulation back into his limbs. He was disappointed but also relieved. Another postponement. The dream could live on without reaching its uncertain conclusion.

Twice more he came back and twice more the fish was a no-show. It was odd, he thought. When he came just to watch the fish it was always there, but when he brought the rod, it was not.

The fourth time he had a flat tyre on the way to the river and by the time he changed it there was already too much light to risk climbing the tree. The fifth time it was almost a routine, all the nervousness gone, worn off by repetition. He fully expected the

THE TROUT BOHEMIA

fish not to be there again and he wouldn't have minded that. But as the darkness faded and the forms of the world materialised out of it, he saw the fish where it always fed, in the eye of the vortex, barely moving from side to side as it took the insects which came straight at it.

Lying on the log above the pool, Richard felt a most disorienting moment of unreality, and he squeezed the cork handle of his rod until his nails bit into the palm of the hand. The pain reassured him. No, this was not the dream again, though everything looked exactly as if it was. This time it was real. This time he would see it through to its conclusion, whatever that might be.

He felt strangely calm; all traces of buck fever had left him by now. There was no fear, no doubt. He dropped the fly into the water below him, then slowly lowered the rod after it, tip down. Supporting his weight on his elbows so he could use both hands, he peeled the line off the reel and let the current straighten it downstream. His leader was short and straight and it had only one knot in it, and Richard had tested it many times.

He glanced at the fish. It was still feeding, unperturbed. The rod tip was nearly touching the water and Richard estimated that the amount of line was just about right. He took a deep steadying breath and let it out slowly, and at the bottom of the breath, with his lungs empty and his mind clear as when he was loosing an arrow from his hunting long bow, he cast to the great fish.

It was a sideways cut, using the surface tension of the line on the water to load the rod, and it sent the fly to the edge of the eddy, too far from the fish.

'Oh crap,' he muttered, but didn't dare to correct it. Any odd movement could alert the fish.

He saw the fly bob there for a moment, bristling and settling, and then the current took and spun it around, into the centre of the vortex.

It was like in the dream again, the fly speeding towards the fish, twitching on the water, and out of habit perhaps Richard suddenly feared he may wake up again. Then the fly was gone, and it took him a moment — just the right amount of time, he later thought — to realise that the fish had taken it.

He struck sideways, a reverse of his cast, and the next few moments were a blur. The strike unbalanced him and he fell down from the log, right hand clamping the fly line to the cork handle to keep it tight, left arm instinctively wrapping around the girth of the log, preventing him from going down head first.

THE TROUT BOHEMIA

If the water was cold he did not feel it. His feet bounced off the bottom a couple of times, a moon-walker's gait, and he foundered towards the bank. The water here was still chest-deep but the footing was good and he held the short rod up, as high as he dared.

The fish was down deep, under the logjam. It didn't run or pull; it just buried down and held. But the line was not fouled, Richard was sure. It felt taut to a breaking point but clear, without any odd vibrations which would indicate a snag.

The short rod offered no leverage so all he could do was to hold on. Every so often a fierce bell-ringer's tug travelled up the fly line and into the rod, but mostly the fish felt still, and unbelievably heavy.

Richard could not tell how long this combat of stillness, this battle of wills, went on but, as the adrenaline wore off, he could feel how cold the water was, and how his body was going numb from feet up. He even considered clambering up the log again, but it was too high and too risky.

'He's waiting me out,' Richard thought. 'He's cold-blooded and I'm not. He can wait all he wants and I'll get stuporous from the cold and then he'll make his dash.'

Richard was shivering hard now and he looked about, but there was nowhere he could get out of the water, not without fouling the line. And then the rod broke, snapping in two at the joint.

He swore, jabbing his hands up, reeling in the slack. He feared that might happen. There was too great a difference in the flex of the rod's two sections: too much in the tip, not enough at the butt. Now, the tip section slid down the line and into the water.

'I'm losing him,' Richard thought. The butt of the rod did not bend whatsoever and all the pressure was on the top guide ring. It was only a matter of time before this would break off too. He had to do something and quick.

He tightened the drag on the reel, then aimed the rod down and along the line, pointing the stub at the fish. Then, with infinite care and feeling, he started to pull, not just with his hands but with his whole body. It felt like withdrawing a long pin from the ground. The gains were small, a couple of inches at a time, and he reeled them in as he leaned forwards to pull again.

Then suddenly, there was no more resistance and he fell back, losing his balance again, feeling the water around his neck, stumbling to regain his footing. With no room to back off he reeled frantically to keep up with the slack line coming at him, and then he saw the fish, floating up to the surface, not moving, not even shaking its head, beaten.

> '*There is no need, and no more excuses, to kill a living thing to put it above your fireplace.*'

Richard had his favourite 'Rusher' net on his back, made from an exquisite mix of native timbers and with a gape and depth big enough for a salmon, and he scooped the giant trout, tail first so that the head protruded above the rim of the net, and it was a feeling like no other.

He took no pictures, never even considered keeping the fish.

'There is a potter in Nelson, Alan Ballard, who is also a fly-fishing guide,' Richard told me. 'He can make you a ceramic replica of any trophy trout that is almost indistinguishable from the real thing. There is no need, and no more excuses, to kill a living thing to put it above your fireplace.'

What he did do, though, was to hook the net to a digital scales he had borrowed for the occasion and the display showed 15¾ lbs. But the fact barely registered.

'From the moment I scooped him up all I wanted to do was to let him go again,' Richard said. And this was where the trouble began.

Removing his own fly was easy enough, but the old spinner dangling from the corner of the trout's mouth proved tricky. It was embedded deep and would not budge, and as Richard did not want to handle the fish too much, in the end he snipped the spinner off with the wire-cutters of his Leatherman, trimming the hooks of the treble flush with the trout's jaw.

It took an awfully long time but throughout all this, the fish was surprisingly still, never once flapping in the net. Briefly, it occurred to Richard that perhaps the fish knew he was trying to help it. Injured wild animals have been known to behave that way. But as he released the fish from the net, holding it by its massive tail and into the current to revive it, he realised it was not so.

The giant fish would not revive.

'He was totally spent,' Richard said, his voice knotting up with emotion. 'I nursed him against the current, pushed him into it,

and every time I let him go he would keel over and float down and I
had to grab and hold him again.'

There was faster, more oxygenated water above the willow choke
and Richard ran there, splashing out of the pool on his knees,
carrying the fish in his arms like an injured child. He held the
trout in the riffle, one hand around the base of the tail, the other
cradling the head into the life-giving flow of water.

'Breathe, mate, breathe, BREATHE!'

When his hands were numb from the cold he let the fish go and
the water turned it sideways, and washed it up against the curtain
of willow branches that barricaded the way into the pool where the
fish had lived.

Richard retrieved the body of the fish, and carried it on to the
bank, and he sat there next to it, and cried.

'It was so tragic. I've never felt so awful in my life. I've shot big
animals and killed fish — this is a part of who we still are, hunters
at heart — but this was such a waste. This old man fish fought till
the end, to die rather than surrender. Sometimes I wish all this
had never happened. But, then, I'm also grateful that it did.'

He buried the giant fish by the pool where it had lived and he
let the trail overgrow again.

All this happened some years ago. There is a new fish living
under the logjam now, nowhere near as big but growing steadily,
feeding from the vortex in the current. Richard has not fished
since that day but he may again some time. For now, he still walks
his home river, and a few times a year, in the still hour of dawn,
he puts on his camo gear and slowly and deliberately, like a true
hunter that he will always be, he crawls up that log above the pool
to watch the new fish.

To watch but not to touch.

chapter 8

'Fly-fishing is not just a way we catch fish, not even a lifestyle. It's a compulsion, it's who we are. It's a way of being and relating to the natural world.'

PJ JACOBS

It was Christmas, the time of merry holidays, feasts and family reunions, when our idyllic and picturesque little town — which branded itself as the world's first lifestyle reserve — endures an annual invasion of vacationers, swelling tenfold in population, becoming, as some long-time residents refer to it, a zoo. I usually leave for a few weeks at this time, letting the so many others have their place in the sun, by the lake and on the river, slices of paradise that we as locals consider normal and everyday.

It was Ella's birthday too, on the last day of the year, and I suggested we go away camping, just the two of us. It wasn't a fishing trip, but I had my gear with me as I always do. I thought we'd go where Ella could swim as she loves to do, and I could fish if we were near good water but mostly we'd just camp, and hike, and read and be together. We had food for a week, and wine, books and a guitar, and we'd start at the Ahuriri Conservation Area which is one of my favourite places, and which I had long wanted to show her. It seemed a good plan for a romantic getaway. What could possibly go wrong? Ella agreed, if somewhat reluctantly.

The Ahuriri is a long and superbly scenic mountain valley which leads off towards the Main Divide, between Otago and the Mackenzie Country. I'd been coming here for years, regularly though not frequently, to fish and hunt, to hike or climb, or to just walk in the elvish forests of beech and tawhai trees. In sun-baked Central Otago where I live such forests are a rare thing, and so from time to time I suffer from an almost unreasonable compulsion to walk in shady woods, especially those of the red beech, with their columnar trunks and clean, easy-to-walk-through understorey. For this I would often come to the Ahuriri.

For decades the entire valley used to be an active farm. There was stock and cow patties everywhere, including the forest, and the ubiquitous 'No Dogs' signs were getting bigger and more frequent the further up the road you travelled. To access parts of the valley asking permission was expected if not quite strictly enforced and it was easy to have an impression of being not quite welcome here, merely tolerated.

All that changed with the expiry of high-country farming leases. On the two large stations in the lower valley the anglers' river access and public easements to the mountains beyond the farmland have been clearly marked so everyone knows exactly where things stand. Beyond the stations, the Upper Ahuriri is now a 49,000-hectare conservation park, dog-friendly, open to the public and offering a plenitude of outdoor activities. With the absence of stock too, the land has been reverting to its wild and untrampled self with every passing season.

Ahuriri is a difficult fishery, the femme fatale of a river that can lure you in with her beauty and coquettish promise, then turn aloof and unapproachable, with the water running stone-blue and opaque for weeks on end, and the downstream wind so strong it can prevent you from even opening the truck doors. Also, because of its reputation, the river is so unhealthily popular on a fishable day it is hard to have a piece of water to yourself, especially during the long Christmas holidays. Run-ins and squabbles just short of punch-ups have been known to occur with predictable regularity here, incited by anglers whose desire for a solitary tête-à-tête with the beauty had been thwarted by the presence of others, equally eager but less chivalrous.

None of this was a concern to me as we drove up the long gravel road into the valley. As I said, this wasn't a fishing trip. The day was perfect and sunny, and the mountains on the western skyline still carried a lot of snow on them. It's a sight that never fails to elevate my spirits.

I parked near the end of the road, by the river with several deep pools, crystal-clear now, good for swimming and even better for evening hatches, all within a stroll from the red beech forest. There was a rocky creek bed coming down from the mountains, waterless now but littered with firewood, the bone-dry branches and tree limbs scattered like pick-up sticks, and the grass was soft and flat, ideal for camping. Like a greyhound out of the gate, Maya raced out to chase after hares and I took in the world around us and thought, 'This is heaven if I ever saw one'.

'There're sandflies here,' Ella said.

'Yes, a few. Want some repellent?'

I had to admit there were more than just a few sandflies, certainly more than I remembered. Perhaps the stormy and wet spring was the cause of it. The grass in the valley was prairie-high and lush, and the bloodsuckers like the moist environment.

The only solution was to cover up head to toes and this Ella was doing now, grudgingly pulling on her safari pants and a shirt, wrapping a scarf around her face like a chador. I could sense that, deprived of her favourite pastime, she was working herself into a foul mood.

'I'm going to find the dog.'

The dog had no trouble finding herself but I could not face another drama and Ella knew it.

Maybe we really weren't compatible, I thought, walking the riverbank, away from the camper. I was a fly-fisherman at heart, a worshipper of places wild and remote, or at least natural, happy to gipsy around from one river to the next, a trout bohemian. I could follow a river for a week, alone but never lonely, delighting in the smallest and often incommunicable incidents along the way: how the sunlight and shadows played upon moving water, how golden willow leaves spiralled into it and formed mosaic patterns in bankside eddies, the way a trout could go after a hatching mayfly and miss it, its jaws snapping empty air below the fluttering insect.

For nearly twenty years I had lived in a small town on the edge of a large national park, among mountains and rivers and lakes, and my forays into cities had become brief and businesslike, in and out, the quickest way possible, the world of malls, crowds and shopping without any allure at all, the snarls of traffic and the noise intolerable. In my bones and blood I could feel what American writer and environmentalist Rick Bass meant when he wrote: 'Perhaps I'm no better than the so-called yuppies [. . .] in that the way they crave money, possessions and security, I crave wilderness.'

It would have been hard for Ella to understand all this. Her idea of the great outdoors was an alfresco café. She had lived her entire life in big cities, embracing their art scene. It was very bohemian too, no doubt, but it was centred on galleries, exhibitions and performances, and the kind of high-heel soirées where you sip bubbly from fluted glasses, discuss latest trends in painting or dance choreography, and try to derive the meaning of life from someone else's brushstrokes. She was a model, talented painter, and at heart, a dancer. For her, an adventure was a weekend workshop of Argentinean tango in one of the big towns. Which would have been fine with me if she hadn't insisted I come along, despite the fact that, as I told her, on a dance floor I felt I had two left feet and the wooden grace of Pinocchio. I guess tango was to her what fly-fishing was to me.

And yet, despite our differences, we had so much in common. She liked my cabin by the river for the same reasons I did. In the world of worshipped consumerism, my cabin was an exercise in deliberate simplicity, and she liked that too. She saw it for what it was, that I was there to make a life not just a living, that it was not a descent into 'trailer trash' lifestyle but the act of letting the extraneous and the illusionary fall away, a decluttering of personal space so that, within it, time and freedom could hold the ultimate priority.

Ella also loved silence as much as I do and disliked any background noise. Have you noticed how silence has become a rare commodity these days, how often people are uncomfortable with

Generic CDC dry fly

the sound of it? Silence is not just the absence of sound. It has a
sound of its own. The silences I treasure most are those of the high
mountains when all noise has been muffled by the fresh powder
snow. These, and the murmurs of rivers which, without being
contradictory, are silence and music both at once.

With this background of the river soundscape in my cabin,
Ella and I spent hours talking about Zen, about realising one's
true nature. How the soul was like a diamond so encrusted with
existential muck and grime it was often unrecognisable for what
it was, merely a dull rock, and how it took a lifetime or more of
deliberate effort to clean it up and make it shine again.

Well, maybe we weren't diligent enough in that, or maybe it was
all insufficient to keep us together. Perhaps Lizelle was right. If
you're not compatible, trying to be together was like connecting a
three-pin plug into a two-hole socket. It just wasn't going to happen.

For the next few days we hiked and cooked, camped and read. Ella
swam and I fished but all the while the tension between us festered.
I took to spending more and more time away from the camper,
walking along river and in the woods.

There was one high moment for me over this time. The river
was beat up from the legions of Christmas anglers trooping
its banks at hourly intervals, each team proceeding with the
unshakable confidence of piscatorial conquistadors about to loot
the Ahuriri's fabled treasures, apparently oblivious of each other's
presence. Most of those I saw or talked to would go home fishless

as the trout responded to this invasion by hiding in the undercuts, in deep pools and under riffles. But the fish came out to feed after sundown, when the valley was empty of cars and people, and even the most persistent of anglers succumbed to the allure or obligations of Christmas feasts and revelries.

This one evening, as Maya and I eyed the long even pool near the camp hoping to spot a rise — although I never taught her, she had developed an uncanny ability to point rising fish the way other breeds of dogs point hiding game animals — I became aware of a low hum just above the ground. It was like being near an active beehive, only that the buzz was of slower and deeper vibration. As I examined the tussock at our feet I saw that it was alive with brown beetles, shining in my shaded torchlight like brass sequins, bumbling about on the edge of the river.

The beetles were everywhere and it wasn't long before the fish responded to this bonanza of easy meat and Maya went ballistic running up and down the bank, pointing the hard splashy rises. I cast a deer-hair beetle imitation and hooked a fish, and it was surprisingly large and superbly conditioned. So was the next one and another after that. By then my sorrowful mood was gone, even giving way to a vain smirk. Where were all the trout conquistadors now?

The beetle windfall lasted for hours and I lost count of time. Normally, I would stop fishing when I could no longer see the takes but there was a quarter moon out and enough starlight to make out the contours of the banks and so to judge the distances. The summer air was still and warm, my deer-hair fly held together well, as did the knots, and since I only rarely had to use the headlamp, my eyes grew adjusted to the darkness. I would net a fish and hold the tippet tight, then run the Ketchum Release along it until the hook remover's grooved tube found and enfolded the barbless fly, and popped it out harmlessly. I would lift the net up briefly, and relish the heft of the trout straining my wrist, then lower and upturn the net, and watch the swirl the fish had left on the moonlit water.

We could not see the rises but we could hear them well. Maya would find them first, and freeze quivering in that classic pointer poise directly across the river from the fish. Thus, with the space where the fish was narrowed down to only a few metres I would wait for another rise and pinpoint the trout with enough accuracy to warrant a cast. It was not sight but sound-fishing, and it was new, unexpected and immensely satisfying.

I lost count of fish too, but they were all good and solid, night feeders educated in the ways of how to survive and grow large on this exceptionally popular river. When all the action petered out I sat on the bank with my legs dangling over the water, uncorked the hip flask and sipped and savoured the fiery malt, the Laphroaig feeling more like smoke than liquid. I wanted to memorise this moment for eternity, and feared what I would find back in the camper.

When I got back it was nearly 3 a.m. and Ella was asleep. I did not wake her.

Beyond the beetle interlude the days that followed were like a deathbed vigil, but eventually we both knew the vigil was over. The Fates, if they were behind it, would be rolling about in laughter at the perfidy of their joke: first they let the two soulmates finally find each other, but only to let them realise that they just can't get along.

The one and a half hour drive back to our little town was one of the longest of my life. The air in the truck was thick with the sense of finality. At home, we were both too stunned to say or do anything. We just stood there looking at each other until I turned away and walked towards the camper. As I got in, Maya gave me a consolatory lick. They always seem to know when you need one.

There was only one thing to do now: to go back to the rivers, to what I knew and loved, to what always worked. The simplicity of river life has a healing quality to it. Nothing much matters there, only the water, food, enough gas for driving and cooking, the weather. There are things you need of course but, by and large, it is not very much. The world's affairs and their urgency are of no concern when you're on the water, and the priorities are different too: more natural. What matters most is waking up before a dawn full of promise, in anticipation of a new day, an unknown river, fresh possibilities. To the uninitiated this may seem repetitive but, mysteriously and inexplicably, it is not as fly-fishing for trout can be a wellspring of endless variety.

The time too, as American author Edward Abbey wrote in his *Desert Solitaire: A Season in the Wilderness* passes 'extremely slowly, as time should pass, with the days lingering and long, spacious and free as summers of childhood'. When I was still guiding I used to tell my clients that, coming from their daily lives of fast pace and hyperactivity into the pursuit of trout, they needed to slow down to the speed of the water they fished. On swift runs and riffles favoured by rainbows you can get away with being hurried, even brusque, but the slower brown-trout water will force you into more finesse and care. In still water, the stillness itself is often the best strategy as, more often than not, you see the trout precisely because they are moving and you are not.

THE TROUT BOHEMIA

Going fishing then, whether for a day or a month, is like an immersion in another universe, a return to the source, where the water rejuvenates and washes you clean, taking away the accumulated muck and grime, and leaving you with only what's essential and true, like a polished river stone, and who knows, maybe exposing some of the facets of that diamond within as well.

I wished I could have shared this all with Ella, but clearly this was not to be. Compromising does not need to be a sacrifice, and in the end, being true to oneself is the only path worth walking, hard as it might be.

Driving away, I found reassurance in the lyrics of a song from the soundtrack of the movie *Into the Wild*, about being alone and better off for it, about becoming best friends with one's *own* soul and not grasping for another. This seemed a kinder destiny.

I briefly passed by my cabin to pack what I needed for a summer on the road. The new light Stalker rods I'd ordered from Australia had arrived, a #4 and a #5, and they were sure to help along the journey towards refinement, in fishing at least. I'd grown to like the brand for its fast action and accuracy. I've had their #6 for years and all the shine was gone from it now, which was exactly how I liked it. The new ones would need a going over with photographic dulling spray until the sun has done its work on them. On a bright day, a rod flash can be as visible as a strobe light or a mirror signal, which makes an angler — who may otherwise be wearing a full camo outfit — look rather asinine, suddenly exposed like an emperor with no clothes. It makes you wonder why, with all the boom in the camouflage gear industry, where not just rifle and shotgun barrels are imprinted with foliage patterns but also fly boxes and forceps, no one's ever come up with an idea of making fly rods that are at least dull if not camo. Maybe they would look less appealing in shops.

With a few emails and phone calls I caught up with people I wanted to fish with and made a plan of action. I'd spend another summer in the North Island, I decided, a month or two at least, and, by fortuitous turn of events, I'd start with the man who claimed to have caught more trophy trout than anyone else on the planet. His methods too were as intriguing as they were unconventional.

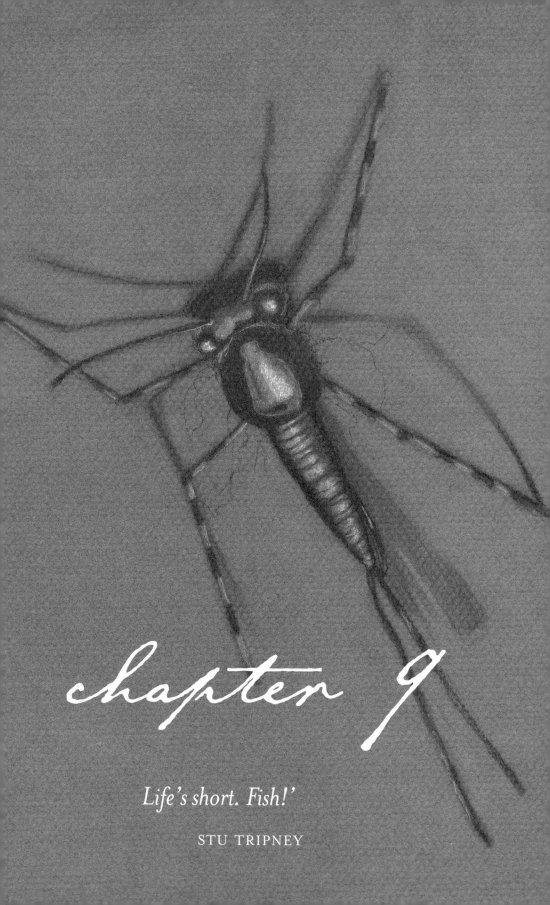

chapter 9

Life's short. Fish!'

STU TRIPNEY

'*Forget* — all you know about fly-fishing. This is a whole new game, like nothing you've ever done.' Miles Rushmer was standing on a rickety wooden bridge spanning a creek narrow enough to jump across, and he held his stout fly rod pointing at me like a rapier. In his other hand, pinched between the thumb and forefinger, he had a dull-grey nymph the size of a small pebble but twice as heavy. As he drew the fly up, past his right eye and then to his ear, the 20-lb tippet tightened and bent the rod into a bow.

'Lesson number one — and two, and three: always make sure the barb is clear of your fingertips,' Miles said. 'If it's not, the moment you shoot, the hook has only one place to go: into your finger. And with this kind of drawing power, it'll go in deep, right to the bone.'

The rod was in his outstretched left hand, the fly by his right ear, his eye sighting down the tippet the way an archer looks down the arrow. Then he loosed the fly and it shot forwards precisely twice the length of the rod, hitting the wooden planking with a thud. It was a bow-and-arrow cast refined to near perfection.

Miles lifted the rod and caught the fly with his shooting hand, loaded up and repeated the action, again and again, showing me the basics of the technique. The rod had to be parallel to the ground, the length of the line set and locked with the left hand pressing it into the cork handle. Fly to the ear, eye sighting down the line. Like in traditional archery, in which I had once dabbled for a spell, form was everything, directly translating into accuracy. And Miles's casts were remarkably precise. If you put a coffee cup down on the ground he would probably hit it most times with his nymph, if not quite dunking the fly inside it every time.

We were in the Bay of Plenty backcountry, not much over an hour's drive from Tauranga. Miles is a happy upbeat kind of guy and if he comes across a little cocksure and irreverent he has good reason to be. Over the past decade and a half, along the ditch that ran below our feet, and in similarly secret local waters, he had been a party — either fishing himself or guiding a client or a friend — to the capture and release of some 500 double-digit trout, mainly browns but rainbow as well. Most of them were caught using the bow-and-arrow cast because in the jungle creeks where the monster fish hide no other technique would work.

Miles had always played the high game. He ski-raced and surfed, and for several years was the editor of a surfing magazine, jet-setting around the country, hunting big waves with the top surf athletes, juggling big-name sponsorships. Then he came to Tauranga to do his post-grad diploma in marine sciences and fell in love with the place so much he has not left it since.

'Everything I love is here,' he said. 'It's truly a bay of plenty. There are beaches and surf, world-class big-game fishing just offshore, deer in the patches of bush within half an hour from home, pheasants and turkeys, and trout . . . man, there are dozens of rivers and spring creeks here, and it's rare to see another fly-fisherman on them.'

The Bay of Plenty is best known for its sea fishing: the 300-lb striped marlins, 1000-lb blacks and 800-lb blues, and for the epic yellowtail kingfish, perhaps the best there is. But what does a marine biologist, a curious and laterally thinking fellow, find when he turns his eyes inland? Endless opportunities, it seems, and all these in places dismissed by most anglers as unfishable. Which is how, by a highly original piece of off-the-wall thinking, mixing deduction, knowledge of the fish and its environmental needs with an extraordinary amount of legwork and disregard for discomfort, Miles has added to the plenty of the bay, the discovery of what is quite possibly the best brown-trout trophy water on the planet. In the bush creeks near Tauranga.

'We knew there were big fish here, and plenty of them, but come summer they all just seemed to vanish,' Miles recalled. 'So we wondered: where would they go? We followed the rivers and creeks all the way up to the headwaters, until they started splitting into tiny feeder streams and ditches completely choked with brambles and gorse, and still we could not find the big fish. And I thought: what if they went further up, right into that jungle?'

It made perfect sense. The water there was shaded all day and so it stayed cool even through the height of summer. There was plenty of food and no disturbances. No animal or human would ever bother the trout.

'Any sensible angler would just take one look at the place and say, "There is no way you could ever fish in there,"' Miles said.

How wrong would they be! How sorry. Miles added secateurs to his fishing kit and pushed on, into the thicket.

'I'll never forget the day we first dropped into this ditch,' he said. 'We had to cut a tunnel through a six-metre-high wall of blackberries and the water we found was one long choke of willows. But in amongst it all there were the big fish alright. Some two dozen brown trout, between ten and twenty pounds, in about a kilometre-long stretch of bush-bashing up the creek. In my whole life I've never seen anything quite like it, and on public water too.'

Of course, it was impossible to fish for these giants, in any conventional way at least, though that did not stop Miles from trying. There were deep pools and undercuts in the creek but no room to cast, no way to fight the fish that were so strong they could spool you on their first run. After a few days of concerted effort Miles and his friend managed to land one fish — a 15-pounder — or rather the fish landed itself. It came out of the water with such ferocity it beached itself on dry land, at which point Miles dropped his rod and tackled the fish to stop it from bouncing back into the water. The entire fight took only seconds.

'When all strategies failed we tried putting a landing net in their way and, no joke, one fish sailed straight through it, and blew the hoop on its way out. I guesstimate he was about eighteen pounds. Unstoppable. There are fish in there probably over the twenty-pound mark — bigger than many kingfish I'd seen. You hook into one of them, in such confined space, and it'll give you a whole new definition of all hell breaking loose. None of our early hook-ups lasted longer than five seconds.'

In the logjams of willows good fishy real estate is precious and so Miles would often find several big fish in one pool. 'Once, I spooked six of them with one cast, their combined weight a hundred pounds or more, and they all turned downstream in unison and came hurtling at me. It was frightening. In such shallow confined water, on the sandy bottom and with the reverb from the undercut banks, they sounded like horses galloping straight at you.'

This talk had taken place the night before, and it went well with the local wine as we sat on Miles's verandah, getting to know each other, planning the next day's hunt. But it all came flooding through my mind again now, as I stood on that old weathered bridge furred with mosses and lichens, learning the combat application of the bow-and-arrow cast, about to drop into the ditch full of the biggest trout I'd ever see.

How many double-figure trout have you caught in all of your angling days? I can count mine on the fingers of one hand. The one in Kahurangi, another in Rangitikei, two on the Coast, the last one in Tongariro — each of them clear in my memory as if recorded on an HD video clip. Imagine, then, crawling down through a bulwark of brambles, like commandos negotiating swathes of barbed wire, needling our way through the willows, not as thorny but just as dense, to come upon a pool, gloomy and dappled with sunlight and no longer than a car, with five trophy fish in it. I had to sit down; Miles, patiently behind, waiting for me to get over the shock.

'I know how it feels,' I heard him say. 'It takes you out, doesn't it? When I first saw them I could not sleep for days. Couldn't wait to get back.'

I would not be getting back here anytime soon I knew. This was a one-off outing and in any case Miles would not fish this creek more than once a week for fear of disturbing it too much. And so for long minutes I just watched, on my knees on the edge of the ditch, feasting my eyes on the sight only a handful of anglers would ever see. Five trophy brown trout, lined up in a formation like jet fighters, which each of them would become if you managed to hook it. For now, they were motionless against the sandy bottom but for the barely perceptible rippling of their fins.

'Here,' Miles finally broke the reverie, handing me the rod. 'Have a go. But remember: there are no rules here. Anything can happen.'

I threaded the rod through the branches towards the pool, and inched my way after it, still on my knees, keeping the lowest profile, judging the distance, drawing the rod into a bow. All excruciatingly slowly, like a predator who only gets one chance to pounce on its prey.

The basics of a bow-and-arrow cast are simple enough but their real-life application is rarely so. There were obstacles all round me, each a potential tangle or snag. Good form called for the rod being parallel to the water and the tip drawn to be up at the right angle to it. Earlier, Miles explained that overloading the rod would cause the fly to go out too hard and bounce back when it got to the end of the line, while underloading would make it drop short of the target. It wasn't aerospace science but a matter of feel and experience, and being new at this game I didn't have either. To make things worse, the water was well below us, requiring shooting down at it, screwing up all my careful calculation of angles.

And then there were the fish, each giant alone enough to give you the jitters, their number and proximity compounding the symptoms exponentially into a dry-throat, leaden-limb paralysis of buck fever. Did I mention, there were more fish around them, smaller ones, like 4 to 6 lbs, each one a decent catch in its own right now dwarfed into insignificance by the big five?

'Don't rush it,' Miles warned. 'You'll only get one cast.'

Cast of a lifetime? This was definitely time for the astronaut's prayer again. The odds were not good.

Finally in position, I sighted down the line, breathed deeply and at the bottom of the breath loosed the fly. Surprisingly, the cast went exactly where I wanted it to go. But something else happened too. As the heavy fly sunk neatly in front of the fish, the tip of the rod — the whole quarter section of it — slapped the water like a whip. My cast was too steep, the angles all wrong.

The immediate effect was as if I had jumped into the pool myself. Suddenly, there were fish everywhere, those we had seen and several more which had shot out from beneath the undercuts, all ricocheting off the banks like snooker balls after a particularly vicious opening break off. The crystal water of the pool turned into instant mud as trout the size of Chinook salmon churned up the bottom, beating it with their muscular tails. God, they really did make that noise: a burst of sound like galloping horses, panicked and wild. Then the pool went silent and still, lifeless.

'Fair go,' Miles chuckled slapping me on the shoulder. 'Wish you could see your face. Text-book shellshock.'

I said nothing, just trying to get my breathing back to normal. My heartbeat felt like a drum machine run amok, my mouth and tongue lined with sandpaper.

'Don't worry, there's no shortage of these brutes in here,' Miles was already weaving his way upstream. 'There'll be plenty more.'

From the outset I insisted that he did not guide me as such but that we fished together. It's always better that way. You not only get to fish but to see how it is done properly. We only turned one bend in the ditch when Miles sighted a single trophy fish tucked right against the opposite bank. Cautious like a stalking cat, he approached it, his rod already loaded and ready to fire.

Then, 'Ah shit!' he said, lowering his weapon.

'What?'

'He knows we're here.'

'Hasn't spooked. I can still see him.'

'Yeah, but he won't eat any more.'

'How do you know?'

'See his dorsal fin?' Miles pointed at the fish. 'See how it flopped down? That's the first sign he suspects something's up. In a relaxed trout the fins are up and alive, like the ears of a gun dog.'

True enough, even as we entered into its window of vision, the fish did not spook in any obvious way. It just slowly drifted deeper into the undercut, out of sight and out of danger.

'They can be such moody bastards at times,' Miles said.

We pushed on. Barely a few more metres upstream there was another big fish, sunning itself where a patch of sunlight hit the sandy bottom through a gap in the canopy. From a low crouch Miles bow-cast the fly and the bomb made remarkably little noise as it hit the water. There were many refinements to the art, that much was clear, including a delicate presentation.

'Ha! Got him!' Miles exclaimed.

He stood up, striking against the heft of the fish, and . . . broke his rod on an overhead branch. The momentary distraction, and the ensuing handicap, was all the fish needed to break free.

'Bugger!' Miles said, examining the damage. 'This is the twelfth rod broken on this creek.'

We only had one rod between us — to halve the tangles in the jungle — and we tried to repair the tip, then bypass it, to no avail.

'It's going to cast like a pig,' Miles pronounced, testing the flex. 'The fishing is hard as it is. You don't need another variable thrown into the mix.' We went back to the truck to get another rod.

An hour later we were back on the ditch and I was beginning to relax into this mode of trout hunting, although this only brought the magnitude of the challenge into sharper relief. It wasn't just the unfamiliarity with the technique and the unforgiving terrain. Our biggest problem was any fisherman's most unlikely woe: there were too many fish in the creek.

We would see a likely trophy, of which there was already an embarrassment of choice, and we'd stalk towards it with utmost care and stealth, only to spook other fish, those hiding in the undercuts, or those we failed to see in the dappled half-light of the creek. These would shoot upstream, causing a domino effect that would empty of trout all water ahead of us, until the next natural break like a logjam, of which fortunately too there was no shortage.

There were plenty of opportunities, but only a few I'd consider as 'fair' — fair to the angler that is, because the odds were almost always stacked heavily in favour of trout. This was, after all, why these great fish were here in such abundance, and why Miles loved this place like no other.

The learning curve in this game of bow-and-arrow trout hunting was vertical. Miles caught a reasonable fish soon after swapping the rods, only reasonable because it was just touching on 10 lbs, and he was now giving me all the shots and, dutifully, I botched every single one of them.

I've never been graced with the so-called beginner's luck. Whatever I do, I always have to earn it, pay the full price, build the critical mass of skills and judgement before anything happens, and it was no different on the ditch. As one snow avalanche expert wrote, in another context: 'good judgement comes from experience, and experience comes from a lot of bad judgements', and that day I would have made the guy proud. I won't bore you with listing all the goof-ups I notched. Suffice to say, all the things you could do wrong with the bow-and-arrow cast I did do, and some of them more than once. Just about the only thing I didn't do was to hook myself with the fly. Lesson one.

Miles just chuckled and said that I was a quick learner. 'The first day is always humbling, the second day is the revenge,' he went on.

Only that we didn't have the second day, not on the ditch anyway. It was now late afternoon and we were slowly running out of water to fish.

And then it happened. We were two pools away from the end of the beat when we came upon a huge fish holding downstream of a partly sunken log, a double-digit with pounds to spare. The water was faster here, slightly broken, and the ripple would disguise the plop of the bomb. After so many failed attempts, the great expectations and even greater disappointments, all my buck fever was gone, my bow-and-arrow casting relaxed. Even my sense of humour was returning.

I cast the heavy nymph deliberately at the log, bouncing it off it in a billiard-style presentation Miles had showed me earlier.

'Perfect!' I heard him applaud. Then, an instant later:

'Yes! You've got him!'

I struck, wary of the overhead hazards. There was a ferocious tug on the line, then, near the log, an explosion of spray. The pool churned into white water, the weight of the fish heavy, and angry, like nothing I'd ever known. Next, Miles was leaping into the pool, net in hand, flailing about, the water level with the chest pockets of his shirt. There were a few moments of total chaos in the confined space below me, and then . . . Ping! . . . My rod whipped back in a self-propelled backcast and the line tangled up in the trees above. Just like that, the great fish had broken me off. On the 20-lb tippet.

There was that sound of galloping trout again. Going. Going. Gone.

'Only when the last tree has been felled, the last

river poisoned and the last fish caught, man

will know, that he cannot eat money.'

CREE INDIAN PROPHECY

THE TROUT BOHEMIA

On the morrow, Miles had another day off guiding and we teamed up to fish the spring creeks of South Waikato. Even if you didn't wet the line in them, the creeks are a delight to behold, gathering from unseen seeps and wetlands, running cold and dizzyingly clear over a stable bottom of cobblestones and pumice, with sandy patches here and there, and weed beds as exquisite as if planted by a Zen gardener. The creeks had been on my To Do list ever since I found out about them a few seasons earlier, though until now I had always been distracted and diverted by other more famous waters nearby: the Taupo region, the Rangitikei, the Rotorua lakes.

Now I had the Fish & Game guide to the creeks with me, which included a map of the major waterways — the Waihou River and Waiomou Stream, the Little Waipa and the Pokaiwhenua — all offering 'many kilometres of fishable waters with good access and numerous trout'. I had also hatched a plan of exploration: the usual quick drive-by to get the bigger picture of the land and its waterways, a sampling from a few different beats to learn about the nature of the creeks, their bug life and trout. Fishing more with eyes than with the rod, at least to begin with, because the network of creeks was extensive, and you could easily spend a couple of weeks here, so how else would you know where to begin.

It was a good plan, although it did not stand up to the encyclopaedic local knowledge of the area Miles had accumulated over the years.

'There are a lot more creeks here than what you see on your map,' he said as we bumped down a single-lane farm road. 'When I first moved to Tauranga and discovered these creeks I promised myself to walk and fish every single one of them all the way to the source, even if it took a week. And this I did so, if you don't mind, we can skip the drive-by part and go straight to one of my best finds. A personal favourite.'

If his other finds were anything like the ditch we fished the day before I wasn't about to argue.

The scenery of the South Waikato is what it's now so inseparably associated with Hobbiton — green and prosperous, a pastoral idyll filled with piebald cows, the volcanic hills unhurriedly tapering off into the distant plains of the Waikato River, misty and fertile. The hills, coming down from the Kaimai Range, are full of nooks and hidden corners, patches of native bush that usually indicate the presence of streams and miniature gorges, places of good structure and stability, shelter and plentiful food for the trout.

Along the single-lane road we met a farmer on a quad bike and Miles stopped to chat, about the weather, the rainfall, the health

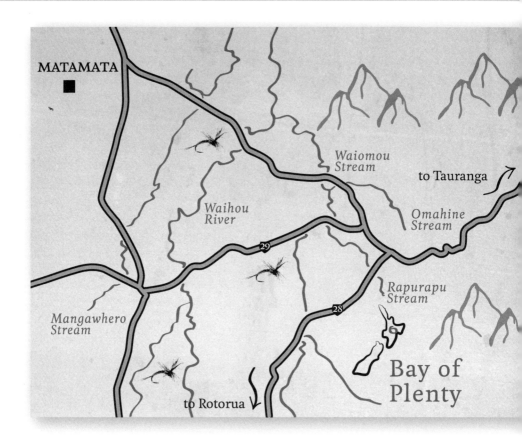

of the farmer's kids. Had the young one got over the wretched flu yet, Miles enquired, and the man said that not quite but the worst was over. Then he waved us off to the creek, mentioning in parting that he saw a couple of good fish just below the bridge, when he was fixing the cattle fence.

We dropped into the creek and immediately upstream, between the walls of what looked more like a rocky gateway than a gorge, we saw our first fish, feeding freely on the surface. The bottom was cobbled with rocks the colour of weathered bricks and against them, and despite the full sunlight glinting off its back, the fish was dark, almost bronze.

'The browns often look like spawning rainbows here, as they key their camouflage off this dark bottom,' Miles explained, then left me to cast.

What contrast in style and finesse to the day before. We were back to 5-lb tippets and #16 dry flies, and I had my new #4 rod out for the first time. It would cast as precisely as throwing a dart, though often, unaccustomed to its lightness and overexcited by the sight of rising fish, I threw this dart only to miss the board entirely.

I did not goof up on this first fish. The tiny CDC split-wing touched down and settled, and it looked damned nigh natural as it came bristling down towards the feeding trout. The fish took it with such confidence you'd think it had never before seen an artificial fly. As we connected, there was a sudden charge of electricity in my hands as if the fly line itself was a live wire earthing high voltage. The fish zapped about like a bolt of lightning, lithe but trapped in the confines of the gorge.

'What a spirit!' I heard Miles cry out. 'I've never seen a fish move so fast.'

This then was my introduction to the South Waikato, the land of spring creeks.

We lost ourselves in the hunt, following the dell through the hilly paddocks, more rocky gaps and pockets of bush, though largely oblivious to the scenery as it was hard to take our eyes off the water. On a creek this delicate, fishing blind would be a travesty and a total waste of time. Spotting was everything — scanning the surface, peering into the depths, always on a lookout for the hint of a shadow, shape or movement that would betray the presence of the trout so perfectly camouflaged, so supremely in its element. The alertness of our senses was so intense, at regular intervals we had to take breaks and breathers, tiring of the concentration yet not wanting to take one upstream step without giving the water our full attention.

Miles caught a fish, then another one, and I netted them for him, feeling that, like a magnet seeking its own kind, I had once again found a fellow trout bohemian, a kindred spirit. He was more skilled, to be sure, more experienced — who wouldn't be after so much big-fish mileage — but his passion for trout and the places where the trout live burnt as bright and clear as mine, and that despite those countless trophies he had caught and helped to catch, which was all the more telling. The creek babbled and whispered its sweet nothings and we walked its banks in comfortable silence, best friends already even though we had only met two days earlier.

The further up we went the more enchanting the creek grew, its course cutting deeply into the land now, the gorges more frequent, the bush cover almost continuous. The fish were not numerous, but they were all good, and they all took dry flies, which made each of them alone worth the walk and the effort.

We sat on a rock overlooking another long and promising glide, and we ate our lunch and drank cold beer, and I thought that if there was a some method of measuring the levels of happiness and *joie de vivre* in my blood the way cops test for alcohol I would certainly be well over the limit.

But Miles was in a reflective mood. 'Man, I've seen this so many times, had so many clients like that,' he said. 'They slaved all their lives, made a ton of money, achieved great things. They followed the role models of the society which says, "You've gotta work hard, save, get ahead". Now, coming up to their retirement, these guys decide it's time to start spending those hard-earned shekels, you know, play again, something many of them have not done since childhood.'

He shook his head, then nodded at the creek below us.

'So they come to places like this, see it, get excited about the trout and the fishing. They take a few steps towards it — towards their dream — and you can see this terrible realisation hits them. Like, "Shit, man, I left it too late". Their hips are buggered, they've got bad backs and bad knees; some can't even get to the river. It saddens me every time but it also strengthens my resolve. To never be like that, to live now, never waiting to live later.'

I wanted to say something equally profound and bohemian, about how there was really only the Now anyway, how the things we coveted and accumulated — tools and toys excluded — were but a ballast that weighed us down. How I was at heart a believer in the Lonely Planet's 'travel light' adage which said, 'junk is the stuff you throw away; stuff is the junk you keep'.

But just then there was a rise in the middle of the glide and it changed the mood of the moment like a gong. I picked up my rod and slithered into the water.

'My turn, isn't it?' I asked Miles without looking back.

'Seems it's always your turn,' he grinned.

'Only on this creek. And only today.'

The water in the glide was deep, periscope depth and then deeper still, right up to the chest pockets of my fishing shirt. I crabbed along the creek-bank wall, rock-climbing with my hands, slow and careful not to send a forward wake that could alert the fish which was rising still beyond my casting reach. It wasn't too far to cast but the trees met overhead and there were branches everywhere, each one a sure snag.

The fish rose again, its bullet-shaped nose flashing briefly as it pierced the smooth surface sending out a perfect ring and, a little hastily, I tried a side-cast, only to get hooked up in a miro tree above. I pulled the line down slowly, expecting it to snap back like a rubber band, but it came freely and as it did so, it brought down something with it. It was a broken-off double-nymph rig, a red Copper John and a generic PT connected by a length of frayed fluorocarbon. I wasn't the first angler to have casting issues here.

The flow in the glide was sluggish and the rises infrequent. Moving up the feed line, I figured I'd better come up closer on the fish for at least one clean cast. There was a rocky shelf just ahead and if I could clamber on to it I would be in perfect ambush position. On tiptoes now, more swimming than wading upstream in the water up to my chest, I got to the rock and pulled myself up on to it, kneeling down low, getting ready for the cast, my eyes scanning the water ahead, looking for the rising fish.

I saw the fish alright, just below the shelf, not a metre away from me. It saw me too and that was the end of that. Looking down on it all from the skyline edge of the gorge, Miles was laughing.

'Got caught out, didn't you? It happens here a lot. You see a fish moving up the feed line and you follow it. But the trout goes below the surface and downstream to restart its beat again and there you are — too close and in plain view. A better strategy, like in still water, is to sit and wait for the fish. Oh hang on! There's another rise further up. Different fish. Go for it!'

Down from the shelf and on tiptoes again, I made my way upstream. My feet found the bottom rising up and turning to sand as I approached the head of the glide. The fish was against the far rock wall, stationary in the well-defined feed line, rising to a fast beat. A 'sitter'.

I picked him off with the second cast, a loud confident take, then the sense we were again watching a streak of lightning in the water, bouncing off the rocky banks.

Moments later, I was releasing the fish, still light-headed and shaky from the action, and Miles was right behind me in the trees when I heard him say: 'Oh shit! Not again!'

I looked up, then followed his gaze along the creek. Something awful was happening to the water upstream. It was turning dirty before our eyes, muddy grey and brown, with long tendrils of muck racing downstream like storm clouds extinguishing clear sky. Within a couple of minutes the kirsch-like spring creek, which never naturally discolours, ran like a river in spate. And the smell! Oh God Almighty. It would make you retch and gag, if you haven't fainted before that.

I got up on the bank and watched in horror. Miles's lips were tight with suppressed rage. 'That's it for the day here, mate,' he said. 'It's a fucking disgrace and they can just get away with it as if nothing ever happened.'

Turning the corner in the creek we saw them: hundreds of dairy cows in one long procession, crossing the creek with their tails already cocked to the side, stopping to piss and defecate as soon as their hooves were in the water. There they stood, squirting out foul liquid ejecta at the creek and each other, looking at us with those stoic bovine faces that are at once indifferent and curious, and challenging, as if it were us who were the intruders here.

'Don't know what it is about cows,' Miles said, 'but every time they cross a creek they have to stop and crap into it. Must be their idea of a flushed toilet.'

'Have you talked to the farmers about this?' I asked.

'Have I what,' he sniggered. 'Don't get me started.'

But I already did get him started and there was no stopping him now. The situation was tricky and delicate, he said. Along the spring creeks like this one there were patches of native bush protected as public reserves, but the best fishing was on private land, much of which was now converted into dairy farms. You had to ask access permission from the very people who were trashing the creeks you've come here to fish.

'Thing is, when you meet them socially, most are genuinely good guys,' Miles said. 'They have young families, huge mortgages, trying to make a go of farming, joining the dairy boom. Many don't actually own the farms, just manage them for absentee investors. This, I think, is at the heart of the problem. When you industrialise farming, you're no longer talking animal husbandry and land care but stock units, returns on investments and minimum cost growth potential. And screw the environment and the waterways.'

He shook his head. 'They have no idea of the damage they're causing.'

The cows were stretched out into a long, slow and uninterrupted horde and the fenced-off single lane that confined and directed them was a steaming morass of fresh excrement. We could not get past the beasts, lest they stampede and this be construed as 'disturbing the stock', and, in any case, the spell of the day and the enchantment of the creek were irrevocably broken. We turned around and hiked back to the truck, me still in shock; Miles, who apparently had seen such riverine mayhem on a regular basis, recovered remarkably quickly.

'When you talk to the farmers, the moment you say anything negative about what they do, or god forbid criticise them, they just totally switch off, just stand there like footballers, arms locked across the chest. You'll get nowhere that way, may as well be talking to fence posts.'

'So what do you do?'

'I try to take them fishing, one at a time, let them see the value of having clean streams running through the land. They may catch a fish, but in any case, they see the stream from the water level, see that it is a living organism, not a drain ditch. Then I tell them: "Do you realise that, litre per litre, this kind of spring water is more expensive than petrol?"

'"Is that right?"

'"Check the price of bottled spring water next time you do your shopping." They usually go: "Oh yeah?" and then get really quiet. You can just about see the cogs in their brains begin to turn in a different way. Next time you go back to the creek you may see an electric fence keeping the stock away from the water. That's how the change happens, not by imposing regulations and fines. People need to understand and, once they do, they correct their errors naturally and of their own accord. It's a game of rising awareness, not policy enforcement.'

Thus in the hills of South Waikato, Miles Rushmer — a marine scientist, a trophy guide extraordinaire, a trout bohemian and an all-around champion bloke — is saving his beloved spring creeks, one farmer at a time. And he needs all the help possible because here, as everywhere else in the country where the dairy boom has exploded, fast-tracked and untouchable, the situation is increasingly dire.

Unless you are a fly-angler, unless you have walked the creeks and rivers and fallen under their spell, seen them in their glory and in their defacement, you might consider all this a bout of eco-alarmism. You may see it as a cry-wolf sentiment of idle trout snobs who, for the lack of anything better to do, indulge their eccentric hobby while the rest of the population is busy making a living, contributing to the economy. But it is not so.

It does not much matter whether you fish or not because it is not about fishing any more. It is about pure water, the most precious of our resources, a necessity of life. Traditionally, trout were considered an indicator species for the health of freshwater ecosystems, a kind of litmus test of the purity of our water. The fact that in New Zealand they grow large and plentiful spoke volumes about just how good the water was. But we are beyond trout indicating anything now.

There is a disease creeping upon this land, slowly but increasingly noticeable, cumulative like arteriosclerosis. We are losing rivers and creeks right across the populated countryside; they are being clogged up by erosion, siphoned off for irrigation, used as drains, trampled and polluted. Being largely a farming folk, New Zealanders revere their land above all. It's the backbone of the economy, the heartland. But what good is the heartland without its bloodstream?

On the list of countries by size, New Zealand is in seventy-fifth place, smaller than Poland, larger than the United Kingdom, but with a population of only four million people. It is also the world's largest exporter of milk products. As I write this, there are some 6.5 million dairy cows in this country (twice that of twenty-five years ago) and, according to David Hamilton, Professor of Biological Sciences at the University of Waikato, each cow daily produces fourteen times more excrement than a human. When you do the figures, this amounts to an equivalent of a human population of 90 million, producing untreated raw sewage, most of which goes into the creeks, rivers and lakes.

Booms are always followed by busts, which perhaps explains their rapacity. As anglers, we may console ourselves that, like all such bonanzas — gold rushes, stockmarket and real-estate bubbles — this dairy boom is also destined to eventually crash. But until the looting and polluting stops, you too may consider taking dairy farmers fly-fishing, one at a time. Infect them with your passion; show them what's at stake. This may be one sure way to stop this finest trout country in the world from drowning in cowshit.

chapter 10

'He told us about Christ's disciples being fishermen,
and we were left to assume . . . that all great fishermen
on the Sea of Galilee were fly fishermen and that John,
the favourite, was a dry-fly fisherman.'

NORMAN MACLEAN, *A RIVER RUNS THROUGH IT*

Miles had to go back to work but I decided to stay in South Waikato for a few more days, to explore the land and the nature of its spring creeks, to get to know their trout. Most of my time I live and fish in the alpine south, the country of big mountain rivers and relatively few spring creeks. There, on one side, you have the year-round snow and 'Sound of Music' landscapes and, on the other, the sun-baked highlands of Otago. These are arid and austere, bristled with lichens and tussocks, and softened only by the seasonal blooming of wild thyme, a thin purple haze rising from the rocky earth. The landscapes are more European there, the seasons as distinct as the ways to fish them.

By contrast, in Waikato and its neighbourhood, you have no doubt of being on a Pacific island, volcanic and lush, humid and warm, almost seasonless. It is a delightful surprise that in this nearly subtropical climate there are cold, life-giving spring creeks, and that they have trout in them is an even greater wonder. This makes the fishing here all the more appealing and unique, an exercise in thaumatology, the study of miracles.

I could have happily spent a week here, or more, but it wasn't to be. As I parked my camper on the bank of the Waiomou Stream, brewed a coffee and fired up the laptop to consult the topo maps and plan my own Waikato campaign, there came a message from my long-time friend and brother-in-rods Michel Dedual, the trout scientist for the Taupo fishery. The Tongariro River, one of the finest rainbow fisheries anywhere on the planet, where the magnificent *Oncorhynchus mykiss* run up from Lake Taupo the way steelheads ascend from the sea, was suffering, as Michel put it, 'from a dire infestation of large brown trout'.

His friend — a fellow trout bohemian and an expert angler — walked a kilometre section of the river and counted some 150 big fish. 'He brought one home, for the smoker,' Michel said when I called him. 'It was huuuuge . . . I mean massive.' Another day, Michel added, the said friend was nearly reduced to tears after an epic but lost battle with what he later described as 'the fish of his lifetime'. Usually, I would take such tales not just with a pinch but a handful of salt. But coming from a trout scientist who handles big fish daily, who commonly downplays his catches and is never prone to outbursts of mucho macho braggadocio, these carried a whole new subtext of sobriety and excitement.

Still, I had just seen my share of massive brown trout and would have stuck to my guns — or rods, rather — to stay in the Waikato and fish its delicate creeks, were it not for one more detail Michel had mentioned: the cicadas were out in all their

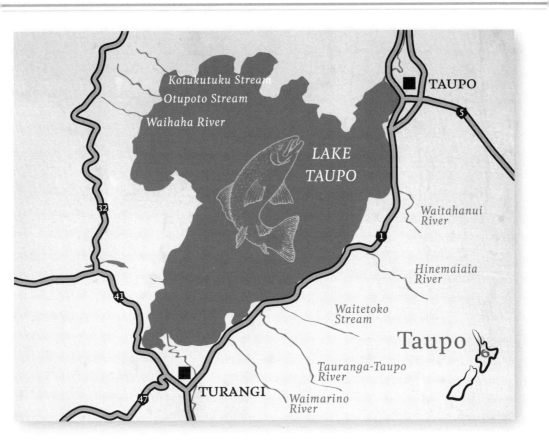

glory, the most welcome of plagues. The noise of their song was so loud, he said, walking through the patches of native bush along the river, you had to cup your hands over your ears, and wished you had brought a set of earplugs. The bumbling insects, as big as half of your thumb, swarmed and sang their love songs, and many fell into the river where the trout waited, motionless in ambush just below the surface.

Like trout, I could not resist the cicadas and the riverside fête they provide so the decision was already made for me. Slapping a fat Deer Hair Cicada against the surface of a tiny spring creek would be an equivalent of throwing a brick into it, sure to spook every trout in sight. But on the Tongariro, the same action was likely to elicit an aggressive response from the fish, an investigation at the least, and more likely a punch-like take. And it was all visual — big, fast, exciting and right on the surface. An unmissable spectacle.

Cicadas are mysterious little beasts. They begin their lives as grain-of-rice-shaped eggs which the female deposits into grooves in the limbs of trees. Out of the eggs, the hatchlings crawl out, looking like termites or small white ants, and begin to feed on the tree sap. After a time, they drop to the ground, burrow in to find roots with more sap for nourishment, and there they stay, depending on species, for between two and seventeen years, unseen by the world and safe from most predators.

After all this time, they crawl back from underground, and climb a tree to shed their nymphal shucks. The old exoskeleton splits along the back of the thorax and the adult emerges with wet crumpled wings and soft new skin. Their wings unfold and dry into shape, the skins harden, and the cicadas begin to sing, each species relentlessly chirping out its distinct song, a precise jingle of accented and unaccented notes, sometimes punctuated with wing clicks.

According to the *Book of Insect Records*, scientists who indulge in such 'work' have recorded the world's loudest cicada singing at 109 decibels, not that far from the maximum intensity of sound the human ear is able to perceive without painful and permanent damage. So, you see, wearing earplugs while fishing at the height of the cicada season is not as silly as it initially sounds.

As winged adults, the cicadas swarm and mate and complete their life cycle which, in places near water, is likely to end up in the stomach of trout coming in to lurk under the trees and near tussocks. A cicada which had fallen into the water can still fly off and that is why the takes are often fast and ferocious. For the trout, cicada season is the time of reckless gluttony, and it all makes for explosive fishing. At least if you can see the fish before they see you.

Like so many times before, I set up camp at Michel's place on the Tauranga-Taupo River and the following day I was on the mighty Tongariro as soon as the cicadas woke up. There was no shortage of fish alright, but there was also one fundamental setback. The weather was a subtropical overcast and it turned the river surface into a pewter mirror, glary and opaque. With no backdrop to shade the water, sight-fishing was impossible. My eyes strained and watered from the effort. They saw plenty of trout but always just a moment too late. You had to be almost on top of the fish to see it, by which time, well, you saw mainly a wake arrowing away. It was more frustrating than not being able to match a hatch, figure out the right fly. You only needed one fly here — the Deer Hair Cicada — it's just that there was almost no opportunity to present it.

When you see fish, and cannot catch them no matter what you do, there is almost a visceral yearning to connect with them, a profound and not entirely conscious or reasonable desire to feel and touch and hold them. I guess this is not unlike the pangs of wanting some guys may suffer ogling shapely supermodels parading the latest swimwear, you know, the kind which gets more expensive the less material it is made of. The world is full of possibilities but you are excluded. And, oh God, how much you'd want to be in.

A few days of this had passed. A lot of fishing but not a lot of catching. With the strategic advantage of the overcast skies those massive Tongariro browns seemed all but untouchable. Frustrated and dispirited, I needed a break. A day in town.

The following morning I drove north along State Highway 1 winding its way north, hugging the eastern contours of Lake Taupo, the largest body of fresh water in Oceania. Under the slab of grey clouds the lake was like a sheet of metal, smooth and without a horizon. Along the drive two unusual phenomena immediately grab your attention. One is the rocks floating on the water's surface — balls of pumice, some as large as pumpkins. The other is the plumes of thick white steam issuing from several places around the lake, the ground there smoking like freshly dug-up hangi.

The nature of this lake provokes sobering thoughts that put not only the fishing but our own existence into a planetary perspective. When you are around Taupo, one of the world's trout fishing hotspots where even the streets have names like Pheasant Tail and March Brown, it is impossible to ignore the fact that the lake itself is the caldera of a volcano whose eruption 1800 years ago was the largest and most violent in the past 5000 years. When volcanoes erupt, their lava, cooling as it flows from the vent, often forms a mountain, sometimes in the shape of gracefully symmetrical cones like those of Mount Taranaki, or more jagged and irregular like the skyline of the nearby Tongariro National Park. But the Taupo volcano never formed a mountain around itself. Each time it erupted, it did so with such violence, it literally blew off its top. The Oruanui Eruption, the largest of them all which occurred around 26,500 years ago and shaped the current lake, ejected some 500 cubic kilometres of debris into the sky and covered islands 1000 kilometres away with an eighteen-centimetre layer of ash.

To really understand Taupo and its firepower you have to find a good vantage point, like the clifftops above Kinloch or Acacia Bay along the northern shore or, better still, the 1088-metre lava-dome summit of Mount Tauhara above the township. Look over the lake and imagine it burning, belching fire and lava all the way into the stratosphere, darkening skies around the world with its ash and smoke, throwing up red-hot rocks the size of cars and houses as if they were sparks from a campfire. But maybe this is asking too much of even the most fertile mind because, from our limited perspective, the forces which shaped Lake Taupo may well be beyond imagining.

Unless you have actually seen it, and — as unlikely as this sounds — there are people who claim they might have done just that.

Q: If a volcano erupts on a faraway island and there is no one there to hear it, does it still make a noise?

A: Ah, but the real question is: was there truly no one there to hear it?

Consider the following passages:

> *Ka hoki whaka muri nga ra . . . and the days went backwards and the night became day, and day became the night. Trees shrivelled up and rocks ran like water. The earth shakes . . . the earth trembles. Terror ran through the land and cried out to the skies.*
>
> *Then the stars fell . . . long showers of flame rained down, and a fiery waka swept out of the heavens. Lightning and thunder raged. Burning rocks crashed to earth. And a frightful humming was heard. And a great burning ball plunged down . . . And the forest burned, and the land burned, and the spirit of Hine Pu Kohu Rangi covered all with smoke and dust.*
>
> *We were saved by sheltering deep within a cave. We waited there for many days for the choking smoke to clear and the Sun to return. When we emerged to the light we found the world changed forever . . . We speak of the Taupo Nui Atea, the huge waka that exploded . . . out of the darkest expanses of space and time.*
>
> *Taupo Nui Atea is a name of awesome power.*

The excerpt is from Barry Brailsford's highly controversial book *The Song of Waitaha: The Histories of a Nation* and relates an eyewitness's account of a catastrophic event which in its magnitude could resemble the Taupo eruption of AD 186, a time when New Zealand was apparently uninhabited. I had the book with me, in my camper's library, perhaps too bulky and precious to carry around on a fishing trip but what better place to read its powerful stanzas than on the summit of Mount Tauhara, or the shore of the lake itself.

The elders of the Waitaha nation commissioned Brailsford
to write down some of their stories which until then were passed
through generations as oral tradition only. They say their
ancestors arrived on these shores at least a thousand years ago, and
that they were not the earliest wave of Polynesian migrations, that
there were people living here already. Being a peaceful folk, the
Waitaha were subdued by the more warlike tribes that followed,
but their whakapapa (genealogy) and their stories survived.

The Song of Waitaha, when it first appeared in 1994, had the effect
of sending throngs of New-Agers reinventing themselves as born-
again Waitaha, and even the open-minded sceptics guffawed with
ridicule. Brailsford himself was at once applauded for bravery,
ostracised by academia, and accused of incompetence and cultural
transgression. It bears remembering though that he was once
a lauded historian and archaeologist, and his early books — *The
Tattooed Land* and *The Greenstone Trails* — to this day remain definitive
classics. Brailsford was even awarded an MBE for his work on
Maori lore before he turned to mysticism and dropped off the
radar of mainstream science. Gone bush, talking to the land, and
the rivers, not unlike so many of us trout bohemians.

Of course, you realise, we are now navigating the frontier of
the unknown, and even more so the very fringe of the acceptable.
Follow or retreat at your peril but keep in mind that it was always
the fringes that most fascinated explorers. Historically, pushing
beyond that warning demarcation line which said 'There Be
Dragons' often yielded the greatest discoveries.

Under other circumstances we might not have given Brailsford's
passages any more thought than we would to similarly beautiful and
evocative pieces of indigenous lore which say, for example, that a
demigod carved out Fiordland with a pointed stick. But then there
were these other shreds of evidence which, if not quite conclusive,
could not be satisfactorily brushed away either.

The solid matter ejected from volcanoes, such as pumice and
ash, is known as tephra. The layers it forms make distinct and
easily recognisable bookmarks in the tome of earth's geological
history. The science of reading these layers came to be known as
tephrostratigraphy and in New Zealand it was pioneered by Alan
Pullar. In the 1950s and '60s Pullar was mapping out North Island
soils, and he developed the science as a sort of weekend hobby.

In 1964 Pullar was called to a dig in Hawke's Bay conducted by
amateur archaeologist Russell Price. The peat around Lake Poukawa
was yielding vast numbers of artefacts — broken and charred moa
bones, stone tools, clear evidence of extensive human habitation —

and Price wanted an expert like Pullar to look at it all and to date it, to confirm or to dismiss what to him seemed unthinkable.

Because, you see, Price had a problem: it was not so much what he was finding but where. Many of the artefacts were buried under the until-now undisturbed layer of ash from the AD 186 Taupo eruption, and some, god forbid, were even below the ash from the earlier Waimihia eruption, estimated to have occurred around 1320 BC.

Pullar investigated but could find no fault either with Price's fieldwork or his conclusions. Now they both had a problem. The world of science likes its horizons gradually expanded, not blown asunder à la Taupo eruptions. And so, in his report to the Archaeological Association, Pullar cautiously wrote: 'If the lower layer is indeed Waimihia lapilli then the discovery by Price of items related to man found below the pumice band raises implications almost too daring to be true.'

In the summer of 1969 a team of geologists from Victoria University was brought in to resolve the matter. Its leader concluded that Price's work was inexpert and flawed, that because the peat was dried up and cracked, the found artefacts must have somehow fallen through those cracks and thus under the layers of Taupo tephra. The case was closed.

But is it really closed or just put into the 'too difficult' basket? The debate continues but I, for one, prefer to keep my mind open and eager. Who knows just what other mysteries may lay buried beneath the layers of Taupo ash?

The contemporary inhabitants of Taupo, many of whom are lifestyle fishermen and women, seem to be taking living on the world's greatest volcano in good cheer. One time I visited, the region's promoters had put on a festival with fire and eruptions as the main themes. There was hot music, spicy food and explosive art, even a host of fire-breathing performers.

Good thing the volcano did not join in the rumble. It may be officially dormant, but the volcanic giant does snore and tremble regularly which is one reason I come to fish here as often as I can, to indulge the lake's treasures while they are still available. If the Taupo volcano goes off again it's likely to make most other eruptions look like puffs of cigarette smoke. By then of course, the trout, best in the world as they may be, will be the least of our worries. But for a brief moment before it evaporates, Lake Taupo would be the biggest bowl of fish soup on the planet. A tureen of bouillabaisse.

Back in town, I stocked up on cicada patterns — a convincing tie with see-through wings, soft rubber legs and beaded eyes, and unsinkable like champagne corks. And a good thing I did because, could you believe it, finally the pall of clouds was clearing from the south. Turangi, at the far end of the lake, was already in sunshine, and the forecast was for a few sunny and cloudless days in a row.

The next morning I was on the river almost too early. The dew was heavy and the cicadas still silent, and I used the time to walk a few kilometres further downstream, keeping away from the river's edge, short-cutting through oxbows, with Maya bounding happily alongside, flushing out hares.

After its tumultuous descent through the hills, gorges and forests, the lower Tongariro is a much mellower river, wide and meandering, still swift but uniform and smooth, favoured by brown trout and more conducive to sight-fishing. There are good evening hatches here too, something of a local secret, though this news is unlikely to break out and lure in cohorts of anglers because the Tongariro mosquitoes are the fiercest I've seen anywhere, including the Amazon and the Kakadu wetlands.

I once made a mistake of camping here, stupidly overconfident in my camper's insect-proof screens. I'm not sure how they got in, and so many of them too, but we were both drained of blood to a point of approaching anaemia. In the end, I had two mossie coils burning on the bench top, filling the truck with smoke, and a mosquito net slung from the roof, and still the little bastards came in in droves, unimpeded. Maya snapped about blindly until the wee hours, and I endured inside the cotton cocoon of the sheets even though it was too hot and sweaty to stay under covers. It was a 'never again' night of hell and only the dawn brought relief from the torment.

But, in the daytime, when the sun is strong in the cloudless sky and the cicadas are chirping, such miseries are easily forgotten. It was about 10 a.m. when I turned around and started fishing back up.

There was an untold number of fish, hundreds of them. Most were out in the open, in the middle of the river, lying in pods of five or six, as grey and nearly as big as salmon, nosing into the rippled contours of the sandy bottom, motionless and totally disinterested in flies. After the initial shock and excitement of seeing so many large trout, and having the perfect conditions for which I had waited for so long, it took me a sobering hour to realise the futility of trying to catch these fish. No matter how much I desired them, they were not feeding and so were untouchable. It was a far better strategy to focus on the first two or three metres of water just out from the bank. There were far fewer fish there but they were all on a lookout for drowning cicadas, motionless too but ready to pounce at the fly. These were not the gentle sips of trout taking mayflies but the KO punches of total annihilation. A sight and sound that make the heart of every angler skip a few beats.

Still, considering this was their time of unrestrained gluttony, the fish were surprisingly spooky. Perhaps living near one of the 'world's trout capitals' had taught them unwavering caution. It was a game of numbers and though the trout were plentiful, the odds were not good. Maybe one in ten would not spook on the initial cast, and half of those would eat the fly. And, of course, on this river, eliciting a take was the easiest part of it all.

The mighty Tongariro, coming down in frequent floods and flowing through soft volcanic earth, had carved a deep moat for its riverbed. The banks are often two or three metres high, and they are steep, soft and crumbling. The water next to them is immediately deep and the bottom a quicksand, so wading is rarely an option. Did I mention trees? A veritable forest of entire willows with root systems and branches, sunk at acute downstream angles to the banks from which they were eroded. A serious boating hazard and a safe haven for trout, which somehow learnt a good number of knots with which to anchor the fly line to underwater stumps, at the same time ridding themselves of the hook.

By mid-afternoon, I connected with perhaps a dozen fish but still had not landed a single one. I lost two leaders, once nearly the whole fly line, and overall I was happy with my progress. All my cicadas were barbless and along the entire stretch I had fished there were maybe a couple of places where you could get down to the water to net the fish, providing you could bring them in to that precise spot.

It was then that I came to a grove of native trees overhanging a calm bay in the river, all abuzz with cicadas. Below, there was a long riffle, the first one I'd seen all day, and there was not a sunken tree in sight. And under the branches, against the sandy bottom below the swarming cicadas, was a huge fish, motionless in ambush. As I watched, a cicada fell into the water, a couple of metres behind the fish. There was an instant stirring in the little bay, as if a toy jetboat did a Hamilton turn at full speed. I heard the snap of the trout's jaws, saw the pale flash of its inner mouth. The wake washed against the banks, subsided, and all went quiet again. The fish was back in its ambush position, motionless once more.

I had to sit down to calm my nerves.

There seemed to be no way to cast to the fish. The tree branches drooped low towards the water, garlands of leaves and cicadas, so even a side-cast was bound to snag on something. I crawled in as close as I dared, considered the options, dismissed them all, then remembered the bow-and-arrow cast Miles had taught me.

He said it was best done with a heavy nymph and almost impossible with a small dry fly but what about a cicada? Slowly, with infinite care, I poked the rod tip through an opening among the branches and pulled back the fly to load my bow.

Twang! My cicada was more catapulted out than shot like an arrow, but it got out a good distance and it hit the water to the side of the fish with an impressive plop. There was a beat of silence as my world stood still, then another one of those jet turns frothed the water in front of me.

I didn't even have time to strike. The momentum of the turn and the take must have set the hook, and the fish felt it, and it tore down the river across that long riffle.

Within moments I was into the backing. The pressure of the current on the line was tremendous, shaping it into a wide downstream arc despite all my efforts to keep it tight. I ran down the bank and into the river, stripping the line, tripping over it, recovering, holding the rod up with my hands outstretched skywards. Against the opposite bank the fish leaped high, shaking its head from side to side. Even at this distance, across most of the river, it looked huge, like a salmon leaping an obstacle. It hit the water with a heavy flop, and then it was up in the air again, an unforgettable sight.

Three times it jumped and each time I held it, lowering the rod as the fish went up, lifting it high again as the trout landed hard, raising an outburst of spray. It all felt like in a trance — doing all the right things without a thought or a fear — touching what the athletes describe as The Zone, the mystical state of peak performance.

Twang!

Coming out of The Zone was much more jarring than entering into it. The line did not immediately go slack, there was too much current pulling on it, but it suddenly felt lifeless. The fish was gone, the trance broken, an act of intense passion interrupted in flagrante delicto. The trout simply spat out the fly which was still attached to the end of the mangled tippet. I tested the knot and it was still strong. The gear held good and I could not think of what I could have done better. I let out a wolfish howl, both a cry of triumph and a wail of loss, and from the bank Maya responded with frenetic barking.

Fish of a lifetime? There was no way of telling. But, man, those barbless hooks! Sometimes I wish I wasn't such an obstinate idealist. I had two more days like this, without potential trophies but still hooking plenty of trout and even landing a few. I was a trout glutton in the season of plenty, overindulging yet being unable to stop myself. But in the end even gluttony must reach its limit. On the third day I realised it was possible to fish too much, to catch too many trout, and that it somehow watered down the meaning of each individual encounter, turning quality into quest for numbers, riverside contemplation into an all-out greed.

An extremely good day's fishing, or three, can leave you in the state of satiety, and, like any big epicurean feast, requires time to digest, to let the experiences settle, because at this point more does not equal better, and you must wait to let the hunger return. There is also a danger, every chance in fact, that the next day will not be as good, just when your expectations have been raised to the highest level. From there, you can only crash down into disappointment and you wouldn't want to do that to your fishing. I found it was best to take my winnings and leave, to change venues, not attempting to repeat or better a good day but treating each one as new and fresh.

And so, while the going was exceptionally good — the best I'd ever known — I left the Tongariro River, its infestation of large brown trout and the godsend plague of cicadas.

A couple of days later, following my trout nose and scant, disparate bits of information, I found myself on a bank of another river which, according to its now largely forgotten legend, was once even better than the Tongariro, regarded by those who fished it then as the best trout river in the country, and the finest headwater fishery on earth. Considering the trout treasures New Zealand has held, the number of rivers and their diversity, the 150 years of stories and fables and uncommonly large fish, even back in the heyday of fishing, this would have been an outrageous claim to make.

Was such thing at all possible? Could there really have been a river better than the Tongariro at the height of the cicada season, or when the winter rainbows were running? And if so, what was left of it?

There was only one way to find out.

The punk-rocker of fly-fishing, Stu Tripney is also Australasia's first FFF Master casting instructor. 'People come to me humbled by fishing on Southland creeks, and I say to them: "I know, it happened to me too. Let's look at your casting, that's a key to fooling these wary trout."'

The slow deep waters of the mid-Rangitikei are dizzyingly clear and enclosed in a papa canyon. After scouting the riffle and the head of the camp pool Mike and Jenny reverted to Tongariro-style double-nymph rigs which proved most effective when the fish were not rising.

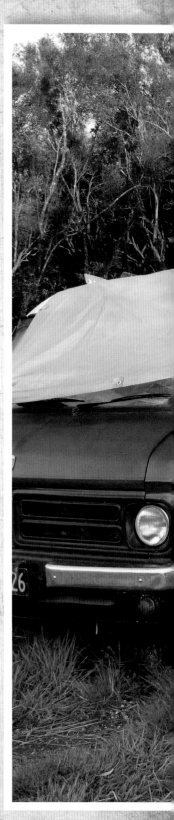

Ralph is a licensed ocean-going mariner and skipper of big-game fishing boats so he knows a thing or two about the right boat for the job. For stealthy prowling around Lake Otamangakau he had chosen a sea-cycle.

The archetypal trout bohemian, Ralph has been coming to fish in New Zealand every year for the past three decades. 'Simple is good, more simple is better,' he says. 'This way there is no stuff cluttering the space between you and the fish, between you and God.'

In fly-fishing there are distinct moments of truth: the hook-up, landing and the release, and Tina and Christian don't miss any of them.

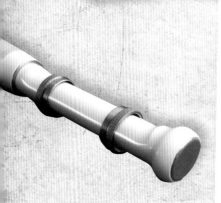

Though they make exquisite bamboo rods, with mammoth ivory reel seats (left) and 18-strip cross-sections (below), in New Zealand, Tina and Christian fish with modern rods and lines, as the backcountry can be as hard on the gear as it is on anglers.

Alone or with friends, on a lookout for rising fish with Maya or 'fly' fishing with Dave Witherow, in New Zealand I too have found my trout bohemia.

Being in love with wild trout can be an exhausting affair. Maya, dog-tired and snatching a power nap while we siege a difficult fish in the West Coast backcountry.

chapter 11

By the calm of a lovely pool, surrounded by the green of giant trees, thoughts rise above the trivia of dislikes and irritations, or petty worries. I suspect that my only worthwhile self-appraisals have been made there on the river in the loneliness of evening.'

PETER MCINTYRE, *KAKAHI*

Dumbstruck! It's the only way I can describe my first time on the Whakapapa River. In my fishing travels I have seen some epic hatches but rarely anything of this magnitude, or precision. Along the white papa cliff, soft like gypsum and overhung with flowering epiphytes, the river flowed with swift purpose, its current forming a feed line no wider than your footprint, and maybe fifteen metres long. Within this narrow band of concentrated nutrients, lined up nose to tail like carriages of a train, two dozen trout were rising, each one porpoising to its own eager beat.

With the first two casts I caught two magnificent rainbows about five pounds each, and they both fought hard, but somehow did not disturb the feeding frenzy of the others. Now, after the third cast, another hook-up and a long-range release, my CDC emerger was chewed up so badly, it would not float any more, and my hands shook too much to change it quickly. I swore, and fished out the bobbin threader, always the last resort in tying on flies because, at a certain age, its use carries deeper connotations. Like giving in to growing old, admitting that the eyes are not what they used to be, and that soon reading glasses may be needed to tie on anything smaller than a Woolly Bugger.

But the hell with it, time was precious. I didn't know how long this first hatch would last and at this rate each cast equalled a fish. I struggled on with the threader, broke its fine wire, swearing while I found a replacement, and all this time across the pool the fish rose to a fast syncopated rhythm; for me, each rise a missed opportunity.

In a flash of belated recall, I remembered how Grandpa Trout prepared for short explosive hatches such as this one. He would have half a dozen flies already tied on and pinned into a patch of foam on his chest pocket, each fly on a half-a-metre length of tippet, the nylon trailing like angels' hair. The knots were tied and tested in good light and the luxury of his cabin, and after each fish he would simply cut off the used fly and put on a new one. This he would do by joining the two ends of the tippet with the triple surgeon's knot, something you could do even with your eyes closed. Thus, no matter how furious and exciting the hatch, his fly changes were always a study in poise and dignity, and each time he presented his fly to a fish, the imitation was fresh and crisp, and floating *comme il faut*, already pre-treated with powder or CDC oil.

'Ah *jeune homme*, you 'ave much to learn, 'uh?' he would say to me, as always, and this time he would be right. But how could you not get caught out like this, an innocent on a new river, confounded by this outburst of a hatch?

There was time for two more casts, and two more fish, equally strong and vigorous, and then, as if some invisible hand had flicked the off switch, the rise had stopped. The fish disappeared, and so did the swallows that hunted the air above the river, and I sat down on a bankside boulder, spent like a runner after a session of interval sprints. Maya nosed in for a pat, her happy eyes and wagging tail saying in unison: 'Isn't this a fabulous river?'

No kidding. The legend was no exaggeration, even if we had arrived nearly a century too late.

Next time, I told her, we would not be caught unprepared. We would not even forget to keep one of those fat fish for dinner. This is how it would be tomorrow, and the day after, and all the other days that were to follow because, I already knew, we'd be staying here for a while. What I did not yet know was that falling under the spell of the Whakapapa, and Kakahi — the tiny time-forgotten settlement on its bank — was a historically documented affliction, and I would be just another angler on the long list of its casualties.

Kakahi, of course, is where the Kakahi Queen and Twilight Beauty flies had originated, where their inventor postmaster Basil Humphrey enlisted the help of school kids to collect undamaged mayfly specimens for him, presumably so he didn't have to do it himself while the fish were rising. Zane Grey fished here about the same time and idolised the place in his *Angler's Eldorado*. Today Kakahi, a scattering of farm houses among green hills at the end of the road, is a place left behind by the headlong rush of modernity. And a good thing too. For an itinerant angler stumbling across it for the first time, settling into its ambience and its fishing feels like coming home, what for a mariner would be finding a save haven after a long odyssey at sea.

Like the Tongariro, the Whakapapa is still a big river even if a good part of its waters is now siphoned off for hydro power. This enslavement had been tactfully done, though, not with a concrete-wall eyesore but with a grate built into the river bottom, much like a street storm drain but big enough to drive through, and it is some consolation to anglers that what water is taken out of the Whakapapa eventually flows into Lake Otamangakau, an equally intriguing fishery.

As big rivers go, the Whakapapa is relatively short. It is born from the union of its two main tributaries Whakapapa-nui and Whakapapa-iti, nui meaning big and iti small. The two rivers come down, cold and clear, from a glacier close to the Crater Lake on Mount Ruapehu, and en route they cut deep ravines through ancient lava flows, tephra and iron-brown ashes. Twenty-five kilometres and some 125 rapids below the confluence of Nui and Iti, the Whakapapa loses itself in the Whanganui, and on they flow together at a much more sedate pace.

Being swift and boisterous, cobbled with boulders and too dark to see into, the Whakapapa is a hard river to fish, harder still to cross or follow any distance upstream. As I was to find out, it's not a place which gives out its secrets easily. Finding good access points takes time, local knowledge, careful enquiries, and often a lot of bush-bashing. And, even then, each of those tracks may only open a way to a pool or two, and above there would be a gorge or a crossing too deep, forcing a lengthy detour or search for another right of way.

The upper section of the Whakapapa is now accessible only by grade 3 rafting as large parts of the river have been 'captured' through exclusive and shady deals between landowners and unscrupulous fishing guides. But around Kakahi the river is still free for all and it still lives up to its legend.

The bankside life is prolific. There are moths the size of monarch butterflies, snowstorms of caddises, and weta as big as your finger. At night, on the forest floor among ferns and mosses, you see myriads of glow-worms, glittering like stars fallen to the ground and in the morning, on the patches of black sand, there are tracks of wild deer which had come down to drink, the imprints so fresh the individual grains of sand have not rolled down into the hollows yet.

The mayfly hatches here have clockwork regularity to them, and the rising of trout is always preluded by swarms of swallows which pick the insects out of the air with deadly accuracy and unbelievable speed. The hatches are short and intense, and once you've sampled their distilled essence, it is easy to forgo the blind-fishing during the rest of the day for it seems to water down the overall experience, like following a glass of fifteen-year-old single malt with a keg of cheap beer. And so, between the hatches, it was all the more pleasant to just be with the river and not fish it, basking in a delicious state of afterglow, coming down from one climax, already anticipating another.

Once you'd figured out the hatch timetable you find yourself with extra hours on hand, and in Kakahi these can be used on extracurricular pursuits, like exploring new access points, getting to know the locals, and learning more about the place and its past and those mythical days when you could stroll to the river and catch trout, reputedly up to 20 lb, on small dry flies.

Many of those now-legendary stories from the Whakapapa

Swannundaze
caddis nymph

River are told in Greg Kelly's classic *The Flies in my Hat*. Kelly was
a retired policeman and an expert in forensic ballistics, one
of the early adorers of the river who, after he succumbed to its
charm, made his life in Kakahi and, more or less, would not fish
anywhere else. But the most eloquent and heartfelt impressions
of the river, both in words and pictures, were left for us by
painter Peter McIntyre, who also came and fell in love with the
place, and built an A-frame cottage and a garden studio on the
papa cliff overlooking a long fishing pool, at the confluence of
the Whakapapa and the Whanganui. To this refuge he returned
regularly and frequently, and from there he worked and fished
until the end of his life. Fittingly, in the act of final closure and
reunion, after McIntyre's passing in September 1995 the river
he revered so much had undercut the papa cliff and claimed his
cottage as her own.

McIntyre was a trout bohemian, scarred and disillusioned by
the atrocities of war. When the Second World War broke out,
the twenty-nine years young painter volunteered for the army
and was sent as an anti-tank gunner to North Africa. There, his
talents with pencils and paintbrushes were recognised, and he
was appointed the official war artist of the New Zealand troops,
documenting their chivalry, and their slaughter, on the bloody
battlefields of North Africa, Crete and Italy.

THE TROUT BOHEMIA

When he returned home, like so many war veterans who had seen too much, McIntyre was in need of healing, and Kakahi — with its river and its nature — provided a nurturing place for just that. He wrote: 'Kakahi has restored my faith in this world as a place to live in. I know every pool on its many miles of river, every track in the surrounding bush. It has been my escape and my hideout from an ever more strident and ugly world.'

McIntyre was a prolific artist and his visual autobiography *The Painted Years* is a tour de force well worth exploring. But for a fly-fisher his must-see book is titled *Kakahi*, a collection of memoir, musing and watercolours.

'Kakahi,' McIntyre wrote, 'especially the country around it and its river, makes a perfect miniature New Zealand; a sort of preservation of so much that was the best in this country, a reminder of a New Zealand that is rapidly disappearing. A place where we could explore and wander, where the beauty and charm were provided by Nature, not Nature organised by man.'

The book is long out of print, a collector's item now. What it contains could easily be receding into the haze of history, eroded from memories by the flow of time the way rivers wash away the evidence of seasons past, were it not for the little dairy in the centre of the village, and the man who runs it.

Manu Lala has the kind face of an Indian sage and a memory like an elephant. He speaks with a strong Maori accent, and recalls fishing with McIntyre as if it happened yesterday. His father Dahya arrived in Kakahi in 1937, drifting in from India in search of a better life, and in the way of Indian traders he started a general store that has been in business ever since.

McIntyre described the shop as 'a sort of Aladdin's Cave festooned with minor treasures of modern life — pitchforks and paperbacks, shirts and spades, newspapers, magazines, fruit and fishing flies'. Today, the shop is still well-stocked with an assortment of practical knick-knacks; anything from tools and chainsaw lube to stacks of canned food, jandals and gumboots, combs and wire brushes, emergency gin and Gore-Tex waders, and the fishing flies are still prominent, good ones too because, after so many years of living by the river, Manu would not be selling duds.

He arrived in Kakahi in 1949 when the Lala family was finally reunited here and one of the first things his father taught him in their new homeland was how to fish for trout on the Whakapapa River. Thus Manu has known the river for over six decades, fishing it through volcanic eruptions and floods, and through its glory years, its downfall and now, its revival. This was honoured by a friend of mine who, only a few months before my visit here, had written a magazine story about the river in which he nicknamed Manu a 'Kakahi King'. This had given me an idea. What better guide could you ask for to fish this river of legends with?

I had been coming to the shop for several days before I deemed it appropriate to ask. Would he show me his river, and, while we fished it, tell me more about McIntyre and those 20-lb trout sipping #16 classic dries?

Manu smiled behind his silver beard. He was polite but reluctant. Yes, at any other the time he would love to, he said, but in just a couple of days he was leaving to visit his family in India and there was so much to do beforehand, with the shop and all, and it was beginning to get quite stressful. Terribly bad timing, really, he apologised.

I considered quoting back to him what he said in that magazine story, how going down to the river was so good because it made him forget about everything else, but in the end I had a better trump card, an unexpected ally. It was Manu's daughter Pramila who was to hold fort here in his absence, and with whom I had been chatting during my previous visits to the store. I'd been telling her how much it would mean for me to fish with Manu, and she agreed it was a good idea. Now, in the decisive moment, she came through with the goods.

'You go bapu,' she told him, 'you've been so stressed about all this travelling, a bit of fishing will do you good.'

Manu giggled and put his hands up in capitulation.

'Can't argue with that,' he said. 'All right. We'll go tomorrow. I'll pick you up.'

And so he did.

He came in late afternoon, after work, and he took me to what he said was one of his favourite and most productive spots. As soon as I saw it I knew I was in trouble. With the hatches that broke out with such regularity I envisaged we'd be fishing dry fly and I had my Ka'ki Queens and Twilight Beauties already Ginked-up.

Alas, no. Manu's favourite spot wasn't even a pool but a fast riffle with clean sheer lines between tongues of current and only small eyes of slacker water in among them. No matter where you'd cast your dry fly it would drag instantly, but Manu was unconcerned about this paranoia of drag-free presentation. Micro drag? What was that? Some kind of reel adjustment?

He had his casts pre-tied, the double nymph set to start with, a double wet — the Ka'ki Queen and Twilight Beauty, of course, but much bigger than mine — for when the light changed. He tied the first one directly to the end of the fly line, lobbed it into the river and immediately had a strike. But he missed it because he was talking to me.

'The fishing here just gets better every year now,' he said. 'As long as we have the water the fish take care of themselves.' Last year, a 14-lb fish was caught and only a couple of days before my arrival a 10½ was landed near this very spot.

In 1972, the same year McIntyre's book *Kakahi* was published, the hydro scheme kicked in and at first it dewatered the Whakapapa almost to the point of killing it as a fishery. Manu estimates that about half the river's flow was drained off and what was left was not enough to maintain the trouts' habitat temperature range. At the height of summer, the pools got too warm and while some of the fish moved out, many more had died off. It looked like the end of the legendary Whakapapa.

But then local conservationist and self-appointed river guardian Keith Chappell took the power company to court, won the case and had the minimum flows restored. Manu had testified at the hearing and ever since he has been a river guardian himself because, as he said, you just can't be too vigilant.

'One day I looked at the river and it was really, really low,' he said. 'I made a few phone calls to rattle their chain and the water came back instantly. It is just not right that someone somewhere miles away can press a button and just like that ruin one of the best trout rivers in the world.'

There have always been some really big fish in the Whakapapa, Manu said, but not all of them trout.

'In them old days there used to be a salmon farm below Kakahi but it closed down, like everything else here, except my shop,' he smiled. 'One time this Maori boy comes to me, all happy and smiling, and he shows me this huge fish he just caught. I took one look at it and thought: this is no trout. So we put it on ice in the shop, and had the DoC people come and have a look at it. It was a quinnat salmon, alright. Gutted, it weighed eighteen pounds and they reckoned when it first got into the river it would have been around twenty-five. That's a big fish.'

I watched him cast. I had never really seen a wet fly fished before, I mean a true wet, that's to say a drowned dry as opposed to the 'wet flies' fished on the Tongariro which are in fact streamers. He cast his tandem rigs across the current and let them swing down, high-sticking the line if it dragged too much. In the fast broken water you would never see the takes, but they were ferocious enough to pull you out of any reverie, if you slipped into one.

Manu fished with practised economy, without a need to prove anything, and he looked happy and relaxed again. Watching him, I thought of what McIntyre wrote in *Kakahi*:

> *I have been intrigued to note how the ways of fishing tend to follow the temperament of the fisherman. Manu, who runs the store and does everything with a quiet restraint, fishes with short casts, never trying to get great distance, never attempting too much, but he moves across the river boulders like a mountain goat, covering every eddy, dropping a fly behind every stone.*

Where did this 'show me how you fish and I'll tell you who you are' supposition leave me, as a fisherman, as a human? Forever the thinker, always needing to learn more, endlessly asking questions, eliminating variables, perfecting the techniques, until everything was distilled into one all-or-nothing cast, the moment of truth like a high-noon shoot-out. This, though intriguing and gratifying to the ego, also had the effect of clouding the mind with too much brainwork, obscuring the simple joy of being on the river the way fast-moving storms can cut off the sunshine.

Manu didn't seem to have these existential dilemmas, this need for answers, the desire for more. He had learnt all he needed to know about fly-fishing decades ago. What he knew worked well and often enough so there was no need to add to it and change or refine anything. This has left him free to fish in enviable contentment, with a faintly beatific smile on his face, his left hand rhythmically coiling the line the way others may handle a rosary.

'It's all about being with the river,' was all he would say, as if even talking about it somehow depreciated the experience. Despite his sixty years on the same river, there was a freshness and innocence with which he fished and watching him I felt a pang of jealousy that, a restless cerebral over-achiever, I couldn't quite relax into it myself. But, then, evolution being what it is, one day perhaps I will.

The day was growing old and we still didn't have a fish, only a few hook-ups without even seeing just what it was we had hooked. I put on a *Coloburiscus* emerger, the biggest one I had in order to give the fish a chance to see it in the turbulent water, and I moved down the riffle. Above, Manu was hooked up again and he hooted with delight, an endearing sound coming from a seventy-year-old.

I cast into one of those eyes of slacker current. The Colly dragged the moment it touched the water so I was effectively fishing an emerger as a wet, and I didn't have much confidence in it.

It was already dark so I did not see the take but I felt it, confident and firm, without any undue splash. Unlike all other fish I had hooked on the Whakapapa, this one did not jump or zigzag around its home pool. After the initial double pull of the take, there was a momentary pause, a recognition of what had just occurred, and then the fish bolted off downstream and cross-current, without any fancy moves, steady but unstoppable.

My reel whined like a dentist's drill and I felt the knot between the fly line and the backing whip through my fingertips.

'That's a beauty!' Manu enthused.

I was running down the bank now, with Manu following.

I heard him giggle: 'Geez, maybe you caught another salmon?'

Unlikely, but what a thought.

'He pulls, man, how he pulls!' Manu chattered excitedly as we tripped and stumbled, running over the river rocks.

I flicked on my head-torch. The fish was across the river and still pulling hard downstream. And you know what? Over the field of boulders, big as Swiss balls and slick with moisture, I just couldn't run fast enough.

In the morning, in my camp on the river's edge, I was scrubbing dishes with the black volcanic sand when I saw a large mayfly eddying out next to me. It was still alive but already keeled over. Big, banded black and sulphur, and floating flat on its side, with the wings folded together and back slightly, it looked exactly like one of Manu's wet flies.

'Use the Ka'ki Queen when the kowhai is in flower,' he told me and I shall always remember that.

An hour later, I went into Kakahi to say my goodbyes, but I was already too late. At daybreak, Manu had left for India and Pramila was on her own in the shop.

Again, we chatted. It transpired that she had only just returned home from London after a ten-year stint there, working as a psychologist, specialising in domestic and emotional violence.

'Like every other psychologist I studied human behaviour so I could sort my own crap first,' she said.

'And have you?'

'It's a work-in-progress,' she smiled.

'Yes, the river has been a constant in all of his life, as important as his business,' she said. 'Maori have a concept they call turangawaewae. It means the place of standing.'

'I could have done with your professional help a while ago,' I said. 'Now it's probably too late.'

'It's never too late if you understand what went wrong and are prepared to learn from it.'

With just a few deft questions over the counter of her father's dairy she had me all figured out.

'Looks like you both understand what the problem is but that's not enough. Some people understand their problematic behaviour perfectly well and still don't change it. Understanding may just lead to more understanding but no real action. People get addicted to therapies too, to talking about their problems, revelling in them. Real change is harder. It requires action and perseverance, and the results are not often dramatic. Just a little progress here and there. But, you know, long-term, one degree change in the compass heading can take you in a completely different direction.'

Indeed. And I thought I came here to learn more about fly-fishing. I told Pramila about our outing the night before and how much Manu was at home on the river.

'Yes, the river has been a constant in all of his life, as important as his business,' she said. 'Maori have a concept they call turangawaewae. It means the place of standing.'

Maori believe, Pramila said, that we don't own the land, we belong to it, and turangawaewae is the place where this connection is strongest.

'This is where you're from, where your roots are,' she said. 'For a tree, this is where the trunk enters the earth, for a human it's a bit more complicated but you get the idea. For Dad, Kakahi has become his turangawaewae and the river is at the centre of it.'

'And for you?' I asked.

'My life is elsewhere,' she said. 'I need to be in a city, work in a big hospital where my skills and experience will be most useful. I haven't yet found my own place of standing.'

I left Kakahi that day but the concept of turangawaewae has been with me ever since. A self-professed trout bohemian may not easily put down roots in any one place but, as Pramila said, it's a bit more complicated than that.

In the past I would never have written about a river like the Whakapapa, certainly would have not named it. In the private and self-indulgent ways of most fishermen I would have kept the knowledge of it secret, for myself and only the closest of friends. But I have learnt, from labour-of-love river guardians like Johnny Groome (see *The Trout Diaries* for his story) that if a river is secret and if it dies through dewatering or pollution, it also does so in secret.

Were it not for people like Keith Chappell, Peter McIntyre and Manu, it is likely that the fabled Whakapapa would not be a trout fishery any more, much less an improving one, slowly regaining the glory it once had. It is more probable that some geek many miles away, with his hands on remote controls, would have pressed the button once too many times and thus dewatered this jewel of a river and killed off its world-class trout without ever seeing the damage he would have thus wrought.

But the anglers stood their ground and this has made all the difference. As fly-fishers, we know rivers better than anyone else. We spend more time with them than any other user, and this time is mostly passed in observation so we are the first to notice changes, whether they are for the worse, or the better.

It seems to me that in this age when our rivers are under so many threats from such diverse interests, when pure water that is clean enough for the trout to live in is rapidly becoming the most precious resource on the planet, the time for secrecy is over. The more of us there are, and the more vocal we become about our passions and concerns, the more valued and known our trout waters and their plight will become. We may lose a bit of solitude in the process but that's a small price if we can keep the rivers flowing pure and free.

As anglers, we are the tribe indigenous to the trout waters. We need to make the rivers our turangawaewae, our place of standing.

THE TROUT BOHEMIA

chapter 12

'To insist that fly-fishing is all about catching fish is
like saying the only reason for sex is procreation. In
essence, yes, it is true, but how much we would be
missing out on if the essence was all there was.'

DEREK GRZELEWSKI

The first time I met them was in my camp on the Whakapapa. They had stumbled across it the same way I did, through good fortune assisted by research and the curiosity to check out new waters.

It was raining hard, the thrum of the downpour on the camper's roof at once lulling and deafening, and Maya and I were pleasantly ensconced inside, me with a coffee and a book, the dog — always using her time with utmost efficiency — soundly asleep at my feet. This high up in the headwaters, even such heavy rain wouldn't amount to much. The river would not discolour for long and it was just a matter of waiting out the tempest in anticipation of it clearing and the next good hatch.

Presently, a green low-slung convertible, its top down despite the deluge, rolled down the access track and came to a stop by the river. The woman in the passenger's seat wore a flowery dress and the kind of hat you may see at races like Royal Ascot or the Melbourne Cup. The man had a thoughtful face and confident bearing, a designer of super yachts perhaps. They were soaked to the skin but seemed irrepressibly cheerful.

I waved a non-committal hello, Maya thumped her tail a few times, and we went back to what the fancy car's arrival had interrupted — reading and sleeping — not giving its occupants any more attention. A couple of eccentric townies, I thought, who somehow took a wrong turn on their way from café brunch to a beau monde garden party. Got lost in the woods, in no country for high heels and designer bonnets.

'The rain and the mud would learn them,' I said to Maya who only an hour earlier refused to go out into the weather herself. She stretched and snuggled in closer, and I again went back to my book.

Next time I looked up I could not believe my eyes. The convertible was still there, now neatly covered with a green tarp and next to it the man and the woman stood remarkably transformed — could you believe it — getting ready to fish. They were both decked out head to toe in the latest Simms' gear, like a couple of models who had just stepped out of the pages of a gear catalogue, but they were stringing their rods with an automated efficiency, something which only comes from having done it hundreds of times. They waved and marched off upstream, rods held forwards, the red pompoms of their Tongariro rigs bobbing with alacrity of purpose.

Now I was intrigued.

They were gone for maybe a couple of hours and all this time the rain beat down as if it was trying to hammer the earth flat. The woman came back with a fish, bigger than anything I'd caught so far, and the man seemed exceedingly happy for her, making a lot of fuss about it and gesticulating praises, acting them out in a way that from outside seemed exaggerated but to which the woman responded with matching intensity.

We chatted briefly, and the rain kept pummelling, and they pulled off the tarp and bailed the water out of the valiant little Fiat, and they drove off, still unable to pull the roof up — the mechanism had jammed open — but this time wearing their storm gear and, as they would later tell me, holding the precious memory of those two hours up as a shield.

What I did not know then was that for them the worst of the tempest was yet to come, and that they were heading right into it. I didn't know that the silly hat Jenny wore was to hold her wig in place — in the past few months she had lost all her beautiful hair — and that from the river she was going straight to another chemo session, and that the prognosis was uncertain, and things could go either way.

A week later I was still on the Whakapapa, settled into a satisfying routine of hatches, reading and work, when Jenny and Mike returned, this time in their fishing 4WD packed for a more in-depth exploration. My initial error of judgement was now laughable, more like a practical joke they unintentionally played on me. They were not a couple of townies lost on their way to a glitterati lunch. First impressions count but sometimes, like selective snapshots, they can offer a false and incomplete picture of the larger truth.

These two were genuine adventurers, an uncommon match of interests and values, in love with life as much as with each other. They had both done a lot of fly-fishing, a tradition that ran deep in both their families, but they could live and play any role, like dressing up for a tux party and changing into fishing or skiing gear straight afterwards.

Jen seemed as comfortable in her stilettos as in wading boots and next to her Mike looked like a guy who was perpetually happy. But wouldn't you? She fished with him, more keen than he was, she taught him to ski, then introduced him to the backcountry and the untracked powder snow that awaited there. She was up for any mission going, whether a fly-in river trip, a World Cup rugby game, or a whizz-bang tour of wineries.

On the Whakapapa, they set up a camp near mine, a big safari tent neatly pitched among native trees and utilising a rocky overhang for a verandah. In front of it, Mike built a cooking fire, we pulled our chairs around it and, as the wine flowed and the flames flickered, there again was that recognition that we were of the tribe and no long introductions were necessary. That evening I heard about Jen's brush with the dreaded 'C'. How, after months of fear and uncertainty, the ebbing tide of her life seemed to have turned within that past week, and how it was again gathering strength, and how she had come to find more of it on the river.

We fished together for a couple of days. I showed them the hatches and they were enthralled to see them, although, as almost all their fishing to date had been done in the heavy Tongariro style, the intricacies of small dry fly eluded them as yet, and so the 'seeing' did not immediately translate into 'catching'. But that would be amended in good time. They were both quick learners and, besides, the world of dry fly is like a cabinet of curiosities filled with fine bone china and other delicate wonders. You wouldn't want to rush in and smash your way through it and they both knew that.

In-between the fishing we talked fishing, and skiing, and the meaning of many things, and so at the end of those two days it felt like we'd known each other for years. In the camp the night before they were due to leave Mike said: 'We'd like to do another river trip and thought of going up the Rangitikei. We've got a jetboat. Could take that.'

It transpired that in her previous life Jen had become a skilled jetboat co-pilot.

'If there's enough water, we could take it all the way up the canyon, right up to the Mokai Gorge,' she said. 'You'd have never seen country like this. Want to come along?'

Is the Pope a Catholic? I had fished the upper Rangi with Marc Petitjean and Michel, but we covered only a fraction of this magnificent river. Below where we stopped, the water was getting too big to fish on foot, the pools ever deeper, each crossing verging on a swim. The only way to explore that section was to raft it down or jetboat up it. As a seeker of river silences, I would have preferred the raft as less intrusive, but between jetboating and no boating on the mid-Rangitikei it was no choice at all.

This is how, one steamy February day, I found myself on Jen's family farm near Taihape, loading my gear into a jetboat that looked like a rocket on a trailer, ready to be deployed.

An hour later we were putting in at the end of an access track

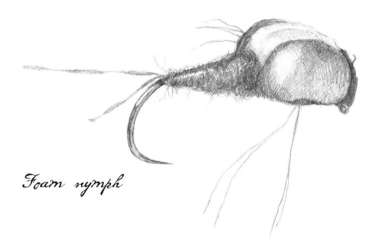

Foam nymph

that wound its way down from the rim of the canyon Rangitikei is so renowned for. No boat ramps here, just terraces of eroded papa mudstone ending in drops-offs into greenstone pools metres deep. Later we saw that the local farmers used tractors with forklift attachments to lower their jetboats into the river. It made sense. Lots of things made a lot more sense later.

The mid-Rangitikei is an intriguing river. The shape of its course is an endless variation on the infinity symbol, bend after bend carved deep into the earth that was once a seabed, and now is a canyon with walls up to eighty metres high. These vertical walls, draped with epiphytes and coloured with iron stains running down them like pottery glaze over the fresh white clay, are soft and unclimbable. Up above, beyond the canyon's rim, it's business as usual and the soundtrack of quotidian life often filters down to the water — the bleating of sheep, the drone of farm bikes, shepherds' curses and the barking of dogs — but at the river level you are in a relative wilderness. There are only a few take-out points, and once you push off into it, you commit to the riverworld on its terms, with all its beauty, surprises and dangers.

Mike and Jen like to travel in style, without excess but with all the comforts of a good safari. Thus our Rangitikei river trip was to be one long picnic interspersed with bouts of intense fishing. We had home-made wine in the form of forty-year-old port (part of their family inheritance), stored in flagons as big as auxiliary fuel tanks and various other concoctions which Jen, a pharmacist, had distilled for no doubt some medicinal purposes. It was just as well we were all in agreement that, when it came to applied medicine, prevention was far more effective than cures. We had enough gourmet foods to make any delicatessen look understocked, and with me and the dog, and all our gear, no wonder the jetboat sat so low in the water.

Mike was concerned about the river level. It was just on the limit of being navigable and he was unfamiliar with the upstream water, though he knew it was quite technical. For jetboaters the Rangi is not as user-friendly as, say, the braided rivers of Canterbury. There, when you make an error of judgement, you're most likely just to run out of water and on to a bank of smooth fine gravel. You relaunch, and try again, and again, without much harm to either the boat or yourself. On the Rangitikei, the game is a few notches more serious. There are cliffs and tight rocky corners, logjams, overhanging trees and boulder fields in fast skinny water, some of them unseen until you are right on top of them.

One downside of Bill Hamilton's invention, about which I didn't know until now, was that everything you did had to be done at speed, ideally high speed. Coming to an obstacle course, like a rock garden in the rapids, you couldn't just slow down on approach and recce your way through. You had to hit it at full tilt because without speed you had no power and thus no steering, and you were at the mercy of the current which could push into 'strainers' like low trees, logjams or cliffs, and hold you there with tons of water pressure. Later, too, I learnt that jetboaters have a saying: 'If in doubt, go flat out!'

No surprise, Mike was excited by the challenge but also visibly apprehensive.

'Let me go for a little scout and a warm-up,' he asked, then roared off upstream and out of sight, although, in the confines of the canyon, we could hear the changing pitch of the jet engine as it powered through the rapids.

He came back satisfied. It was borderline but doable, he said. We just had to go judiciously, one rapid at a time, and be prepared to turn around or camp when the water got too low. Jen mentioned that we'd be better off having a roll cage, but in my jetboating naïvety I took that for a joke.

We jetted off upstream, the three of us standing side by side, holding on to the grip bar just above the windscreen and often leaning over it, towards the nose, to keep the stern up and the boat on the plane. With an outstretched hand to point out looming hazards, Jen navigated Mike through the chaos. I just hung on, and at the back, Maya rode the pile of gear as if it was the tray of a slaloming farm ute, leaning into the corners, her nose working the cascades of wind and scent.

Each turn was like a tall doorway opening up more canyon ahead. At this speed the obstacles came at us like charging bulls and, like a seasoned bullfighter, Mike took them on with deft turns and contra-turns, gunning the motor between the encounters. It was like a bullfight and, high on adrenaline like a good corrida crowd, we applauded each of these veronicas — when the toreador swirls his cape over the bull and spins around — with a loud *Olé*!

Travelling at this white-knuckle pace it was difficult to judge the distance we covered or even the time it took, but our wild ride ended in a long pool into which the river poured over a wide rocky shoal.

'Better not try to get up this one with a fully loaded boat,' Mike said.

'No need,' Jen piped in. 'We can camp here. Look, it's a perfect spot.'

We pulled the boat on to the bank and built a rock anchor. Mike was examining the blue paintwork of the hull.

'That was easier than I thought,' he smiled. 'Only a few dings. Let's set up the camp. And go for a fish.'

The fishing would prove surprisingly difficult. Unlike its headwaters, a renowned trophy fishery where large and challenging trout can be sighted with relative ease, the mid-Rangitikei contains a lot more smaller fish but, because of the nature of water, they are impossible to see unless they come right up to the surface. A typical river section, bending from one omega-shaped corner to another like the one around our camp, would have long shallow riffles or rapids strewn with boulders, ending in diagonal shelves over which the water plunged into pools of dizzying depths. The pools, like miniature lakes, were smooth and calm, but deep along both banks and all the way through, so wading even a metre into them was rarely an option.

This created some serious casting issues. You could bomb the head of the pool right off the shelf using a Tongariro-style rig and both Mike and Jen excelled at that. But when there was a hatch the trout rose in a thin feed line right along the cliff and, without being able to wade in, this was often just outside our casting distance. You could, of course, muster all your skill and power, and send the whole fly line — right into the backing — out across the river, but the accuracy was compromised and, with all the line on the water and across current, the drag was instant and made a mockery of the attempt.

This was most evident, and frustrating, with the trout we came to call our 'camp fish'. As soon as the wake of the boat subsided, and the calm returned, even before we had our tents up, a good fish began to rise right across the river from us. There was a little nook in the cliff there and the fish held in it, sipping dries from the endless feed line flowing right past its nose.

No matter what we did, taking turns at casting with our varying set-ups, we could not get to that fish, or when we did, the fly would not stay in the feed line for long enough, or at the right time. Eventually, one of us would put the fish down, and we would leave it alone, until it started rising again, always a sight that made us reach for the rod and try anew, despite almost assured failure.

Jen nymphed out a fish from just below the drop-off, Mike grilled it over the glowing coals of the campfire, and I learnt that grey driftwood was softwood, good for starting a fire, but for cooking you wanted the brown stuff which was much denser and heavier. This was hardwood which burned even when wet, and it made better and longer-lasting embers to cook over. From then on, even the coffee I made with the billy water boiled on those glowing coals had a smoky flavour of totara.

Every dusk there was a reasonable evening rise and we always fished it, and caught a few medium-size fish and lost others, and then we usually went back to the campfire and the task of lessening the boat's ballast which Jen had brought in the form of flagons filled with home-made wine.

With the jetboat now emptied and sitting much higher in the water we could go up a few more rapids. We would park up above a riffle and fish up until we could not cross again, and then go back to the boat and leap-frog up to another stretch of unfished water. It was an awkward strategy but the only workable one. The canyon scenery was a definition of enchantment, the company some of the best I'd known, and the fishing — hard as it was — became, well, peripheral.

After two days, and several daily assaults, our camp fish was still feeding unperturbed. But I had hatched a plan for him. As we came back from another up-canyon sortie and eddied out in the camp pool with one of those oh-so-stealthy Hamilton turns, I suggested to Mike that we leave the boat in the water and tie it off on a long rope. An hour later, our fish was rising again, unsuspecting that the odds had changed.

Casting from the stern of the boat, though only a couple of metres closer to the feed line, gave Mike all the advantage he needed. He hooked the fish on his second cast, a rainbow of

The river blurred past. The shoals were like washboards and we rattled over them, Jen's outstretched arm again pointing the deepest way through.

about three pounds, but fresh and feisty, a flash of quicksilver in the green depths of the pool. It was a tantalising riddle pleasantly solved and we let the camp fish go. The place just would not be the same without him rising there.

The closer we got to leaving the more anxious Mike was becoming. He had made an improvised river gauge — no more than a stone cairn — and noted that since our arrival the river level had dropped nearly three inches. Not much but in jetboating this could mean the difference between scraping through or getting stuck. Going down was harder too, he told me, harder to see the underwater obstacles and to pick a line through them. And everything happened at twice the speed — that of the boat and the river.

Finally, there came the time to go, and with the dog riding the stern again, and the ballast flagons as empty as we could make them, we pushed off into the pool.

'Well, we can always walk the boat down the rapids on a long rope,' Mike said, more to himself than to us. Then he gunned the gurgling V8 motor, the boat tilted forwards and we shot down the camp pool, towards the white fangs of the rapid below.

The river blurred past. The shoals were like washboards and we rattled over them, Jen's outstretched arm again pointing the deepest way through. The canyon walls came hurtling towards us, then veered off at the last moment as Mike spun the wheel this way and that, allowing for the sideways drift of the boat, in what on a car race track would have been a controlled skid. The throaty roar of the engine echoed off the walls and again we applauded each deft manoeuvre with a jubilant *Olé*, at times ducking under overhanging branches which threatened to take us out.

I had never been in a car accident, but I thought this was what one must feel like: the sudden loss of control, the sound of metal groaning, scraping and tearing, the slow-motion helplessness of waiting for the impact.

Despite the initial trepidation our descent was going well. Half a dozen more rapids, a few of those figure-of-eight turns through the boulders, one or two glancing blows off the rocks we did not see, and we'd be home.

'Shit.'

Mike said it with such calm that for a moment it did not register that something had just gone irreparably wrong: that we were no longer planing over the water, that the river had taken a sharp right-hand turn and we were still going straight, at full speed.

Then, suddenly, there was no more water under the hull, only rocks and boulders, immovable like trees. The boat ploughed on up the bank, ricocheting off the rocks, juddering like a car hitting a row of speed bars. I felt Maya slam into the back of my legs, then glimpsed her vaulting over the side, abandoning the doomed ship. I had never been in a car accident, but I thought this was what one must feel like: the sudden loss of control, the sound of metal groaning, scraping and tearing, the slow-motion helplessness of waiting for the impact.

But the impact did not come. When all the commotion stopped we were several metres from the river, beached up the rocky bank, the smear of paint from the boat's underbelly marking our tangent trajectory like a blue afterglow.

'Bugger!' Mike said, his voice as calm as before.

'Everyone all right?' I asked, hearing the trembling in my own voice. Jenny laughed.

'Derek, I never thought your face could turn such a pure shade of white,' she said.

From a safe distance, wondering perhaps what the hell we did all this for, Maya was watching us suspiciously, also shaking from the shock.

We got out and assessed the situation. We pushed and shoved and tried to rock it, but the boat would not budge. Ever practical, Jen looked around then said: 'We can camp over there. And, it's lunchtime anyway.'

It is always amazing how sudden calamity or danger can bring out resourcefulness and unity in people, galvanise them into action, help them to find strength and skills they mightn't have known they had. I experienced this a couple of times while mountaineering. Upon any do-or-die or how-do-we-get-out-of-here situation, once you accept it, a remarkable calm descends. Solutions seem aplenty, decision-making intuitive, strength steady and plentiful as if coming from some auxiliary fuel tank you didn't know you had, and which only kicks in at times of extreme need.

On a hunch, I found myself playing Archimedes, the 'give me a stick long enough and I shall move the earth' guy. While Mike and Jen began unloading the boat, ballast and all, I climbed up a terrace and found a stand of dead manuka, the trunks five or six inches in diameter, perfect to act as rollers. We dragged them down and made the sturdiest of them into levers. There was no shortage of boulders to use as fulcrums. Thus, inch by inch, we turned the boat around, put more rollers under it and our combined weight and strength to the levers.

During rests between pushing, grunting and slipping on slimy rocks, Mike explained what had happened. 'We glanced off a rock just before the corner and the impact lifted the stern above water. Not much but enough for the jet intake to suck up air. In that instant I lost all power and steering.'

Jetboats are great when all is going well, Mike said, but they can be temperamental too, especially in tricky low water. One small thing goes wrong and before you know it, you're on a self-rescue mission.

'Sounds like a woman I know,' I wanted to say but shouldered into my manuka pole instead.

'One, two, go! One, two, go!' On and on we muscled the unwieldy craft closer to the river.

Our progress was geological, like a glacier moving over the bedrock. It took almost half a day, and two more lunch breaks to get the boat afloat again, although it was still a few metres from water deep enough to attempt to use the motor. Removing some of the bigger rocks from in front of the boat, we made a launching channel and the work was easier now, the progress more rapid.

It was at this moment that from around the upstream corner a posse of burly blokes in rugby jerseys and yellow life jackets came floating down; a group of local farmers who, I noted pointedly, knowing the river levels, had opted for whitewater kayaks and left their jetboats at home.

They eddied out next to us and the alpha male among them got out of his boat. He took in the scene, especially the long afterglow of blue paint, turned to Mike and asked deadpan: 'Did she drive?'

It was a mean jab but Jenny let it slide.

With so much muscle power at our disposal now, it took only minutes to relaunch the boat into a full and deep current and then up into slacker water where we could load up again. Back in their kayaks, the farmers bobbed down the current, dancing through the rapids of their home river, laughing and bantering, no doubt already polishing up a new pub-room tale about three townies who tried to jetboat up the canyon wall.

We followed them, but our relief was short-lived. Two pools down the motor conked out, spurting a rooster tail of steam from the damaged cooling system, and the maws of the last rapids with cliff faces coming up were not a place to deal with that. I leapt out and Mike threw me the long anchor rope, and I walked the moody beast down the last of the white water while on board Mike used the oar to push off obstacles.

It was twilight by the time we winched out and sat on the rocky shelf by the water, drinking the last of the ballast, nursing bruised shins and plucking out splinters, thinking and saying our farewells to the Rangitikei, already dreaming up another adventure.

A day earlier we had seen an oared raft float by, manned by a guide and a fisherman. The craft was made by a Taihape company, Incept, no doubt tested and refined on this very water, and it seemed much more appropriate here than a power boat, going at a leisurely pace, softly glancing off rocks and cliffs, silent and stealthy, much more a fly-fisherman's craft than a jetboat could ever be.

'This is a fantastic river,' I said to Mike and Jen, 'the most spectacular one I've ever seen. But you know what? Next time you should do it in rafts. We'll go with the flow, not against it, at a more natural velocity.'

They both agreed and we made plans, but little did I know that the concept of natural velocity was soon to acquire a whole new meaning for me, and not just in fishing and boating.

I was about to meet Ralph, the ecclesiarch of Lake Otamangakau.

THE TROUT BOHEMIA

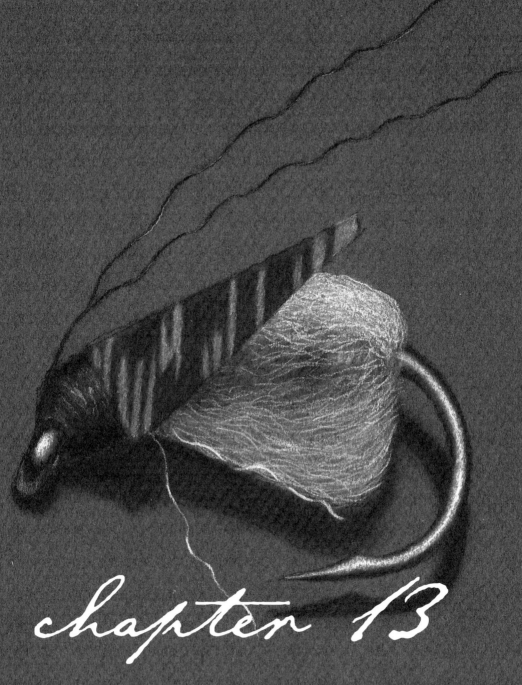

chapter 13

'We fished until we learned that fishing is not about killing or competing or even appreciating nature. Fishing is about being alone on the other end of a line plugged into eternity.'

JANNA BIALEK, *UNCOMMON WATERS*

New Zealand, as The Trout Bohemia, has its doyen and archetype in Ralph, with his Papa Hemingway beard and bearing and his 1970s green Bedford van that looks like a well-lived-in house on wheels, and his sea-cycle. When you consider the Otamangakau fishing boaties as motorised traffic, with their own rush hours, queues at the jetty and races to the best fishing spots, then among them Ralph is a commuter on a recumbent bicycle. Sipping his morning coffee out of a lidded thermal mug he cycles out into the lake, pedalling unhurriedly with a steady cadence, nearly silent but for the swoosh of bow waves from the twin fibreglass hulls.

Ralph doesn't walk much any more, a lifetime of big-wave surfing in Hawaii has exacted a heavy toll on his body, but in his sea-cycle he is a formidable angler. The boat is like two Coast-to-Coast kayaks joined together with a balsa and fibreglass platform. On the deck there is a high seat, rowlocks muffled with wraps of rope, and a fly rod always at the ready. There are strips of carpet where the oar blades rest on the hulls, and no metal chains, no clunking, nothing that could create noise. Instead of an outboard there is a small boat propeller powered with a crank wheel and pedals, as silent as a potter's kick wheel. Everything on board is designed for stealthy and inconspicuous fishing.

'I've got eleven outboards at home in Hawaii and a 28-foot power catamaran called UFO, which is half-boat, half-airplane,' Ralph told me. 'When I come here, I wanna fish without the noise. I often see trout swimmin' on the surface between the hulls and they are not alerted at all, as if the sea-cycle was an island of weed or somethin'.'

The day I arrived at my old Otamangakau camp now occupied by Ralph, I found him exceedingly happy. That morning he had caught a 9¾ and a 10½-lb rainbow, his best for this season so far. I was happy too to meet him when I did, because it turned out these were his last two days on the Big O before an annual tour of the south. There, he would fish the salmon in the mouths of the east coast rivers, the lakes of the west, and spend the rest of his time chasing the world-record monsters that inhabit the Tekapo Canals, some of which he knew so well he had given them names.

'I caught Brokejaw, the twenty-two-pound rainbow, a couple of times, always on a snail imitation,' he said, 'and there is Gulpa, about forty pounds, whom I saw but could never catch so far.'

Thus the timing was perfect, again inspired by Michel who told me I simply had to meet this guy. I did not have my boat with me this time, but with a seadog like Ralph this would not be an issue. The sea-cycle could be fitted with an extra seat. We could fish his last two days on the lake together.

Ralph had been fishing Otamangakau for some thirty years now, which is only about a decade less than the lake had been in existence. This February, on the hillsides around the Big O, loggers were mowing the pine plantations which had reached maturity and Ralph remembered these very pines being planted during one of his early seasons here.

He had lived a big life: won pro-surfing contests, played in a rock-and-roll band, sold his paintings, twice had been told he would never walk again, raised a child as a solo parent. He showed me pictures of his home, an old church lost in the tropical greenery of Kauai, more like a tiny jungle cabin turned into a museum of old game-fishing tackle. Like Ralph himself, it was a relic from the old frugal surfie days now swallowed up by the condo bonanza of Princeville.

Ralph first came to New Zealand for a surfing competition, and touring the island afterwards stumbled across Lake Otamangakau. He caught a fish here with a telescopic spinning rod and saw a fly-fisher casting, and he was so intrigued he went into town, bought the cheapest fly-fishing kit he could find and came back to teach himself the art. He had been coming back ever since, spending a few weeks here each season, refining the art to the level bordering on sublime and, almost as a by-product of that, catching an untold number of large fish.

His best here was the contender to the biggest trout ever caught in Lake Otamangakau which stands at 18.5 lbs. 'I had cheap scales, so not very accurate,' he told me. 'My fish was between seventeen and nineteen pounds. Will never know for sure.'

In 1992, the cicada year, he saw an even bigger fish here, over 20 lbs perhaps. 'Someone had thrown an apple core into the water and as it drifted about it attracted cicadas,' he recalled. 'They kept landing on it until the piece of apple was a little cicada island. Fish were following it and feeding on the cicadas, and I caught the smallest one of them, and it was twelve pounds. I've spent my working life as a commercial fisherman so I've got a pretty good eye for fish size. I reckon the biggest one was over twenty pounds, but we couldn't catch him.'

What you also need to know about Ralph, his lifelong infatuation with big fish and the eye for their size, is that, in his other off-season life, he runs big-game fishing charters off Kauai's North Shore. He also skippers his UFO on coastal scenic tours and takes tourists to see the big waves, 'to get them scared silly' in what he says is like jetboating but through some of the world's biggest surf. It's all Go! Go! Go! seven days a week, an overdose of adrenaline and stress, and so when the tourist season ends he comes to New Zealand for rest, solitude and silence, and what he says is the best trout fishing on the planet.

Some of my most memorable trout action ever took place along the margins of Lake Otamangakau (see *The Trout Diaries*) and so, predictably, I couldn't sleep in anticipation of fishing this very water with Ralph, who perhaps knew it better than anyone alive. But the moment we started, at first light when the lake was but a mirror reflecting the woolly cloudscapes, I realised I had to reset my ideas of what it was going to be like, drop all expectations, relax into Ralph's way of fishing, and living.

With him, there was none of the impatience to cover as much water as possible, and to be the first on it, since this directly translated into more opportunities. As an ocean navigator, Ralph drew himself a map of the lake with all the channels and weed beds marked on it, a map so correctly detailed even Michel was impressed just how favourably it compared with an aerial view. From years of trial and error Ralph knew exactly which spots would fire up when, and so we worked our way around the lake according to this timetable, voluntary subjects to natural velocity.

At first I felt restless, almost disappointed that, here with the master himself, we were blind-fishing the channel drop-offs just like everyone else. But then Ralph caught a fish, and another one, and they were both as good as any I'd ever hauled out of this lake, and this made me pay attention. Besides, being in Ralph's company I could not help but relax into his gentle ways. His unhurried calm, competence and quiet joy were infectious and, as if by resonance, readily available.

This kind of fishing, without the pressure to sight trout and to stalk them, lends itself to companionable conversations. Over the course of the day, we discussed everything from conspiracies and human consciousness, to Illuminati and Christian fundamentalism, the differences between a flamenco guitar (which I toyed with) and a Hawaiian slack-key which Ralph played, and the nature of the Occupy movement which was then in full flower.

'People should Occupy their brains first,' Ralph said, then pointed out to the boaties ploughing deep and noisy wakes across the lake. I was to learn that if there was one thing that could shake Ralph out of the Zen-like state the fishing induced in him, it was boating foolery and incompetence.

'At home, someone wrote a book called *I've Never Met an Idiot on the River*,' he said. 'Good read but the guy obviously hasn't fished a helluva lot. Look at these clowns! Boat out of trim, motor out

CDC spent spinner

of tune, driving right over the fish, spooking everything in sight. Man, they should make this lake "non-motorised boats only". It'd improve the trophy fishing, and the experience of being here.'

Just then, a shiny new boat approached and stopped not fifty metres from us. Splash! Clang! Out went the anchor followed by the burst of machine-gun rattle of the steel chain against the aluminium hull. Oops! Not quite right. The deckhand pulled the anchor up again, the chain against the hull causing a ratcheting racket that under water must have carried around the whole lake.

Ralph cringed at the noise, then started reeling in.

After another splash, clang and rattle, the weekend boaties settled and cast out their fly lines, each with a yellow-orange indicator as big and buoyant as a drowning canary.

'You could mistake one of these for a buoy and try to tie off your boat to it,' Ralph sniggered. 'Let's move. This place has had it for the day.'

He pulled the anchor rope out of the jam cleat and began

pedalling, and we moved off silently like a ghost.

Ah, but it wouldn't be as easy as that. Ralph, you see, is a renowned Otamangakau celebrity, an expert who, though often unacknowledged, is always worth emulating, even if not quite openly. Whenever he moves to make his way to a new spot, other boats mysteriously weigh their anchors at the same time, more quickly and noisily than Ralph, obviously in a hurry. Suddenly, they all seem to be heading off in different directions, but once Ralph parks up again, they materialise within shouting distance around him, with conviction and certainty that they were always coming to fish here; it's just that he beat them to it.

'I'm a magnet for wallies,' Ralph said and shrugged. What could you do? Just keep fishing, knowing that the wallies had less patience and would eventually leave us alone, though at the moment this was unlikely considering the rate at which Ralph was catching fish. With all the accompanying leaping and splashing we couldn't keep that quiet.

It was a treat just to watch him fish, with his #2 rod, 3-lb tippet and barbless hooks, challenging the trophy Otamangakau fish, giving them every opportunity to get the better of him. He was remarkably gentle with the fish he did hook; he had to be considering his gear.

'I can't give the fish any stick 'cause a two-weight ain't got no stick to give,' he laughed. 'Anyway, you don't fight the fish, you dance with it. You get to know it, it's an encounter. It's the only way you can interact with it, feel its power and spirit.'

Often, after the hook-up and the initial run and jumps, he would drop the rod tip down and let the line go slack. 'Now that I've seen the fish I give him another chance to unhook himself,' he said. Unless the fish was worthy of the scales he'd rather not net it but let it get away. By then, he already had the best of it — the take and the electrifying first run — and the rest was but a mechanical necessity, hard on the fish, and thus to be avoided if at all possible.

His rod was twenty years old and irreplaceable, with all its shine matted by the sun and the cork handle taped up to keep it in shape. It was a nightmare to cast any distance, but because the way Ralph anchored the boat and let it swing around on the breeze, we always fished downwind and this helped the casting.

In this kind of fishing, Ralph said, each cast was like a question we posed to the larger reality. And then we listened and felt for answers. The gap in-between the question and answer, the silent pause of anticipation when all was possible, was — according to Ralph — the reason we fished.

'If you study the Scriptures closely you realise God was a fisherman too. That's my take on it anyway. So this is my daily communion, and this . . . is my direct line to God.'

At heart, he was a fundamentalist Christian, versed in the Scriptures but not dogmatised by them, and he considered organised religion — not the faith, just the religion — nothing more than a control mechanism for the masses.

'You don't need an intermediary between you and God,' he said to me. 'If you study the Scriptures closely you realise God was a fisherman too. That's my take on it anyway. So this is my daily communion, and this,' — he rubbed his thumb and forefinger together, feeling the fly line with immaculate sensitivity — 'this is my direct line to God.'

Clearly, the line was sound and the connection good because although the catching was slow, or at least it seemed so to an impatient mind like mine, at the end of the day, Ralph had several good fish, a couple of them around 8 lbs, and I had one beauty just over six. The fishing could not have been more different from the trout-sighting quest I was on during my previous visit here, but I found myself thinking I could really get used to this style, this kind of daily communion.

At the end of the long day Ralph pedalled us back to camp. There were people there already waiting for him, regulars and greenhorns, even guides with clients whose faces were still lathered with zinc sunscreen despite the overcast. They all came to talk fishing, to recap the events of the days, to see what went wrong and what could have gone better. Even the wally newbies with the clanging anchor were there, asking just why they didn't catch anything, and what was the magic fly we had and they didn't.

In the crowd gathered around the green Bedford with its lean-to tarp verandah, Ralph — an abstinent unlike the rest of us — was the elder of the angling tribe, giving freely of his wisdom, listening thoughtfully and patiently to the very people who drove over and spooked his fish. He was like the grandfather we all wished we had, wise but not imposing his wisdom, letting it rub on you, by osmosis and through tranquil hours spent fishing or talking around the campfire, allowing you to make mistakes as make them you must, but then guiding you to an understanding so the mistakes did not have to be repeated.

At sixty-seven, Ralph had nothing to prove and a lot to give. A few times over the years Maori kids in trouble came to learn to fish from him. Some were at a crossroads in life — to follow the gang path as it was expected or to find another way — and maybe the fishing with Ralph helped them to make a better choice.

Ralph knew a lot about fishing, uncommon stuff that only comes from years of intelligent observations. He knew, for example, how the fish had to adjust their eyesight when the light changed from daylight to night, and how this took around forty minutes — far longer than for a human eye — and that in this transition time, they would only take big black things they could see. How the full moon affected the caddis hatches (four days after full was best) and how catching a fish was an act of intimacy, how fly-fishing for trout wasn't an addiction, not even a quest, but an immersion in the great mystery.

We fished together most of the next morning and then I helped him to dismantle the sea-cycle and put it up on the roof of the Bedford. Then we said our farewells and, as it befitted a tribal elder, Ralph had some parting words of wisdom for me too.

Life had its own natural velocity, he told me, and no amount of impatience, of rushing or pushing things along would change that. You couldn't rush a sunset, or a hatch, you could only be there to witness and experience it in its own time. Fly-fishing taught us that, among other good things. It kept us plugged into the larger reality.

A couple of weeks later, I was back in the South Island and heading for home when I got a text from Ralph: 'Yee haw! Just landed a 30+ lb rainbow @ tekapo canal.'

I noted that he still hadn't upgraded his scales.

chapter 14

'If people don't occasionally walk away
from you shaking their heads, you're doing
something wrong.'

JOHN GIERACH

It came in one big crate, over six metres long and weighing half a tonne. As Dave Witherow hoisted it into his double garage in Mosgiel, near Dunedin, it was hard not to think of the package as an oversized cocoon from which something beautiful, light and free was about to emerge. As with most modern kitset aeroplanes, the Courier came with its skeletal fuselage already assembled but the rest of it was in some 800 parts, along with a step-by-step manual.

Over long evenings and weekends Dave pieced the machine together, assembling the wings and fitting the fuel tanks into them, installing the 65 hp engine, running steerage cables over their pulley systems. Finally, some 700 hours later, he trailered the aircraft, with its wings off but ready, to the Taieri aerodrome for its first test flight. Tucked under the pilot's seat were his fly rod and his fishing vest.

Technically speaking, the plane was a cabined microlight, a rug-and-tube design, which in the parlance of backyard airmen means Ceconite fabric heat-shrunk over an alloy frame. Ceconite, taut like a drum skin but so strong that if over-shrunk it can warp the metal frame underneath it, is the same material now used in restoration of vintage biplanes like Tiger Moths. In fact, Dave's plane has the distinct feel of a Moth. And like the Moths in their glory days, kitset microlights have breathed new life into recreational aviation.

'They've brought us back to the days when flying was an adventure,' Dave told me as we walked across the farm paddock in Balfour, to where his Courier was staked out against the wind. 'Microlights are superior to planes like Cessnas and Pipers, and they are relatively cheap. Anyone can put one together, and mine costs thirty-eight dollars an hour to run. Better still, you can land them just about anywhere.'

He ran an affectionate hand along the Courier's propeller, then began his pre-flights checks.

Dave built his plane specifically for 'bush flying'. His idea of a good weekend is to pack light and fly into one of the old deer cullers' airstrips in the backcountry, and to camp under the wing, fly-fish or hunt, returning home with a good look at the country below.

Poet Brian Turner, acclaimed as the literary voice of Otago, had dedicated his book *Into the Wider World* to Dave Witherow, a tribute to some forty years of companionship and wilderness adventures the two men had shared, most of which centred around fly-fishing and trout.

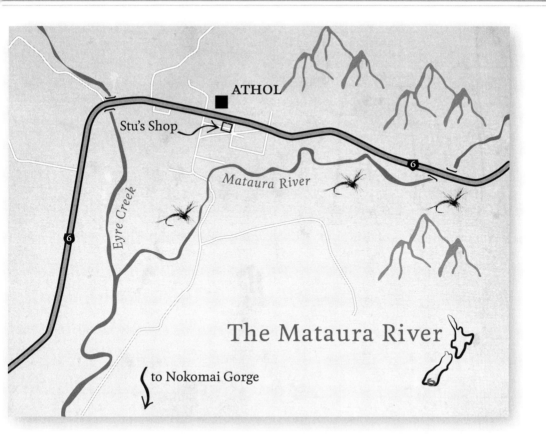

But over those years Dave himself had developed a distinct writer's voice, and as a self-declared armchair philosopher, environmentalist and Fish & Game councillor, he uses it mainly to address the issues of our troubled relationship with the natural world. He is a fierce Irishman, outspoken and proud, freethinker and nobody's fool. He never passes up on a good fight if there is one going and the cause is worthy, be it a harebrained power scheme, dirty dairying, or the protection of wild landscapes and rivers.

'You can't stop the so-called progress, but you can slow it down,' he told me. 'Some of us have to play the role of brakes, or this happy-go-lucky economic circus careers out of control and crashes sooner rather than later.'

I did not want to think too much of crashes as we took off into the clear Southland sky, staying low above the ground, as is customary among the bush pilots. The plane felt more like a double sea kayak that had sprung wings and a cellophane shell over its cockpit, but it motored valiantly through the still autumn air, defiant of gravity and the world below.

'This is the way to see this country,' I heard Dave's voice in my headset. 'People don't realise the beauty and freedom that comes with this sort of flying. Once you're outside controlled airspace, you are free like a bird. The sky is yours in every direction. And there is a lot of sky over Southland and Otago.'

I too had been infected with the bug of flying, which was but one reason I sought Witherow out. Once, on a magazine assignment about Kaikoura — our kind of maritime Serengeti — I took my first flying lesson at the local aeroclub with its own one-teacher flying school. It was intended as no more than a graceful way to finish the narrative, flying off into the sunrise as it were, but instead it was a revelation of sorts. That morning, as Karen Blixen did in the movie 'Out of Africa', I saw the world with the eyes of God.

The teacher's name was Tahlia, freshly out of aviation school, and she gave me an introductory briefing — this is the plane, these are called ailerons, you use them for steering — and moments later I was taxiing on to the runway. She let me do the take-off and then most of the flying, always ready to muscle in a correction with the dual-control steering. She also periodically made radio calls to declare our position, and to my ears this sounded like music:

'Delta Julia Whiskey. Blue Cessna 150. We are three miles east of the peninsula. 1800 feet. Tracking south.'

Later I took some more lessons and contemplated getting a full licence. But, after the initial exhilaration of flight, the pursuit became an expensive and pointless hobby. The aviation rules are incredibly restrictive and to do anything less pedestrian you really need your own plane. Something like Dave's Courier seemed ideal.

As we flew on, following the courses of his favourite rivers, Dave showed me some of his landing strips, some big enough for a 747, others more like oversized helipads. Often a row of wind-break poplars and macrocarpas provided an extra challenge, calling for a dive-down approach. 'With this one, you have to sort of side-slip into it,' he said, then executed an aerial equivalent of a handbrake skid.

The plane did a sharp ninety-degree turn but its momentum carried it forwards as if we did not turn at all. However, the machine was losing speed rapidly. At just the right moment, Dave straightened back and the rubber wheels touched the grass. For a few seconds he rolled along, then he throttled up and took off again.

We continued this hedge-hopping, which no uniformed instructor would ever teach. This was bush flying at its finest and most precise and it was clear that Dave was more at home here than he would be within the sight of a tarmac runway.

'I used to land here too,' he said, pointing the aircraft down towards a small patch of grass fenced in by trees, 'but I can't with this plane. This machine just doesn't drop out of the sky as well as my old Avid Flyer used to.'

'Maybe it's a good thing?' I offered.

'Not always,' he said. 'Sometimes you may want to get down quickly. But the four-stroke motor is definitely better. The Avid was a two-stroke and it used to cut out at most inopportune moments.' At seventy-two, Dave concluded he was getting too old for this kind of excitement.

Still, there was no shortage of exhilaration without the need of adding any more. This was an Icarus-style experience. An edge of vulnerability heightened the senses and flooded them with aliveness, and I felt the old passion for flying rekindling within me, like glowing embers of a campfire fanned by a breeze.

But you remember what happened to Icarus! It was just as well, I thought, that prior to our outing I took time to enquire about Dave's skills as a pilot. Kevin Ireland, who is also a part of the same poetry-and-fly rods coterie and who was staying at the same anglers' safe house Dave owns in Balfour, told me something to ease my disquiet.

'You can trust Witherow's flying,' he said. 'In his misspent youth he got to fly Harrier jets for the Irish RAF.'

As we flew, at minimum altitude, the oblique autumn sunlight shone with laser intensity and it bathed the land below in such beauty and detail, it caused an almost visceral ache. In the modern world of fast and easy travel, where the need of jetting from one place to the next often destroys the simple pleasure of journeying, I was again reminded of natural velocity, this time the one of a bird in flight.

But we didn't come here just for the landscapes or to ruminate on the dream of flying. The hidden meanders of the Mataura at Nokomai Gorge are a prime brown trout habitat and this makes the river one of Dave's favourites. With a bit of practice, it was even possible to spot the fish from the air, the bigger ones anyway. They did not become alert, probably considering us as a big but harmless bird. In this, of course, they were wrong because we had come here as predators.

Hopping over a hedge of poplars, Dave put the Courier into another handbrake skid, rapidly bleeding off speed, correcting to alight on the ground as if he was landing a helicopter. Only then did I notice that my hands were gripping the seat in front of me like a pair of vices, the knuckles white, ready to burst through the skin. But Dave was already unbuckling his pilot's harness and worming out of the tight cockpit.

'Let's go find some fish,' he said, pulling out a rod tube.

We did. The April day was still and clear, as if sculpted out of crystal. Dave, who is as intense a fisherman as he is a pilot, whipped the riffles with his double-nymph rig and was soon pulling out one fish after another. I sauntered off upstream looking for dry fly and finding it too.

The day had ended all too soon, but on the flight home, which I'm sure Dave had deliberately timed with the golden hour of sunset, I again found myself dreaming of flying. Forget helicopters with all the elitism they evoke. Microlights were the way to do it. If only to fly-fish like this, if only to fly with fishing for an excuse.

Ye shall cut betweene Michelmas & Candelmas a fayre staffe of a fadome and a halfe longe and arme great . . . of hasyll, wyllowe or aspe, and soak it in a hot oven, and set it straight. Then let it cool and dry for a month and, in the same season, take a fair rod of green hazel, and soak it even and straight, and let it dry with the staff. Take a plumber's wire that is smooth and sharp at one end, and heat the sharp end in a charcoal fire till it is white-hot, and then burn the staff through with it, always straight in the pith at both ends, till the holes meet.

Make the rod fit into the staff, and to make the other half of the upper section, take a fair shoot of blackthorn, crabtree, or juniper and bind them together neatly with a cord of six hairs, with a loop at the top to fasten your fishing line on. Thus you will make yourself a rod so secret that you can walk with it, and no one will know what you are going to do. It will be light and very nimble to fish with at your pleasure.

And if the angler catches fish, surely then there is no man merrier than he in his spirit. Thence it follows that angling, as good recreation and honourable pastime, is the cause of a man's fair old age and long life.

ABRIDGED FROM A TREATYSE OF FYSSHYNGE
WYTH AN ANGLE, BY DAME JULIANA BERNERS,
PRIORESS OF A NUNNERY NEAR ST ALBANS,
AROUND AD 1450.

THE TROUT BOHEMIA

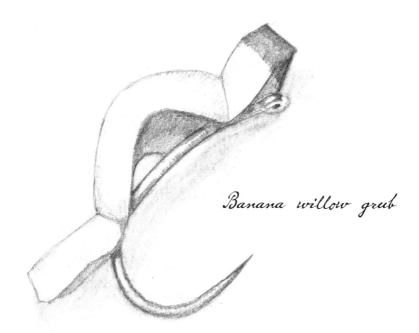

Banana willow grub

My trout-mobile, the go-anywhere Land Cruiser camper, had long been a subject of admiration and coveting by fellow trout bohemians. I've had it for years now, and so forgotten it being any different, but the truck's sturdy appearance and practicality still precipitates a steady stream of windscreen mail, business cards and notes with words to the effect 'if you ever want to sell it, call me'. I never had, and never will, though I felt the same pang of desire when I first saw Tina and Christian's vehicle. Next to it, my Cruiser looked like a tinny Citroën Deux Chevaux.

Theirs was a four-wheel-drive Unimog, custom-fitted and converted into a mobile fishing cabin. I walked around it, feeling its tank-like solidity, and kicked the tyres that reached up to my waist. Now here was a house truck a trout bohemian could retire into.

Tina and Christian have been coming to New Zealand for every season in the past decade and a half, first invited by Norman Marsh whose treatise on our trout insects and the ways to imitate them is still unrivalled today. Early in the game, they had shipped the truck over and kept it here ever since, a home away from home, a mobile basecamp in the land of trout.

I had known about them and their Unimog and, as the truck is one of a kind, when I saw it on a Southland campground, I did one of those Dave Witherow turns and went up to meet them. There was again that tribal recognition which by now no longer surprised me. For hours, we talked fly-fishing, places, river and flies, and people we knew, instantly comfortable in each other's company.

But the surprises were there alright. Though I had heard much about them and their fishing exploits, I never knew that Christian, if terribly modest about it, was a world-renowned maker of traditional cane rods, and that Tina was a casting instructor who could really put those bamboo masterpieces to good work. An even greater surprise was the fact that they had with them a range of these rods which Christian had brought over to demonstrate at a fly-fishing conclave.

I have always considered bamboo rods a nostalgic anachronism, on a par with vintage cars and Tiger Moths, which take more time to maintain than to use. I mean, why sputter to a river in a Model T Ford if you can in style in a Land Cruiser?

There were more practical considerations too. New Zealand being what it is — islands on the edge of the world surrounded by the not-so-pacific ocean — is notoriously windy and a honed ability to cast into the wind, which always seems to blow in your face no matter where you go, is an instant hallmark identifying a consummate angler among the accidental ones. Besides, a modern fly rod — fast, precise and engineered from Kevlar, titanium and carbon fibres — surely had to be superior to a noodle fashioned from a 'fayre staffe . . . of hasyll, wyllowe or aspe' and horse hair with a white-hot plumber's wire.

These then were the ideas I harboured about cane rods, before I tried the ones Christian rigged up for me on the lawn of a Southland campground.

The first impression was just how delicate yet powerful and responsive they were. All the rods were strung with modern fly lines because, for a cane-rod never-ever like me, going straight into silk would be just too confusing.

I cast one of them after another, until I'd gone through all four, then went back to the first one, with each round feeling more of the difference in their performance and speed. They were all as accurate and precise as any rod in my hand-picked arsenal, but there were distinct differences in their personalities and inclinations. One was fast and restless, all its energy in the top third, and I thought it would make a prefect dry-fly rod, while another was slow and smooth, the power travelling all the way up from the handle to the tip, ideal for fishing a shooting-head line. The other two were somewhere in-between, but I liked them all.

Here and there, Christian and Tina offered thoughtful tips,

but otherwise they just watched bemused, seeing again in another bamboo neophyte the dawning of understanding just what casting with a modern cane rod was about. Delicacy. Soft power. Natural ease. Sheer delight.

There was another aspect to the rods, a pure tactile pleasure of touching them, of running your fingers along their polished handmade perfection, caressing the varnish and the mammoth ivory reel seat, something I only ever felt fondling a handmade guitar or a wooden longbow, or a piece of artisan pottery, but never any of my fly rods, or my Land Cruiser. Maybe it was the difference between art and craft, the machine-assembled and the handmade. Both were utilitarian enough, but one was lifeless and indistinct among its ilk while the other had presence and character, almost a personality, as if it was imbued with the maker's soul, their love for what they did.

The tip section of Christian's rods was as fine as a matchstick yet flexible enough to bend into a semicircle. You needed a magnifying glass to see that it was actually made of six identical slivers of bamboo, cut, glued, polished and varnished into seamless unity. Art imitating life or improving on it?

'I come from a family of wheelwrights,' Christian told me. 'For generations we made wooden-spoked wheels but gradually went out of business with the proliferation of rubber tyres.'

He hung about the workshop as a kid and developed a passion for working with wood.

'In a way, I wish I had done a full apprenticeship in wheel-making. There is a lot of demand for such work now and not many people with skills to do it.'

Still casting his cane rods, I was secretly glad that he hadn't. Let the rubber meet the road, let the wooden wheels stay in museums. Let Christian make more rods like these, even if they start at around 1500 euro a piece.

The raw material for all of today's best cane rods comes from one location, Christian explained, the bamboo groves along the Sui River in the Tonkin Gulf, north-west of Hong Kong. This Tonkin cane has the highest density of fibres of any bamboo, and much of it grows impeccably straight and without branches, with well-spaced nodes.

The bamboo tubes are opened, flattened and split lengthwise — split, not cut — following the natural run of the fibres to preserve their full strength and flexibility. Each strip maintains its wedge-shape profile and these are then glued together, most commonly in a hexagonal design, though Christian is currently the only rod-

maker in the world using an eighteen-strip pattern, where each
of the six wedges consist of three strips of pure power fibres. This
adds extra durability and soft strength, and delays the appearance
of 'set' — a downwards bend in the cane rod caused over time by
the weight and fighting power of the fish. (Rotating the rod 180
degrees along its axis while landing a fish is a common strategy to
avoid the set.)

The wedges are bound with cotton cord and heated in an oven
— just as Dame Juliana advised — until the strips align with each
other and the kinks are all straightened out. Unbound, they are
further planed into a taper, then assembled and glued together,
the glue residue removed and polished up when dry.

The resulting sections of the blank rod then undergo a series
of further refinements: sanding and polishing, planing with
a blade sharp enough to shave with. Then come the ferrules
connecting the sections, line guides, the cork handle, the reel seat,
the mandatory leather tube, altogether representing often over a
hundred hours of detailed workmanship.

'Don't rush with orders,' Christian laughed as we were putting
the rods back into their tubes and my hands still lingered over
them. 'I can make only a few a year and I'm booked out for the
next eighteen months.'

Maybe it was a good thing too, I thought. Fishing with such
rods would have to be reserved for the most perfect of days, the
rare occasions only. It would be like sipping an eighteen-year-old
single malt out of a crystal glass on a balmy summer sunset in the
river camp. You wouldn't want to overdo such things.

For the next two days we sight-fished a Southland river together
and these were some of the most memorable outings I had that
season. My companions were both intense and serious about their
fishing but relaxed about it as well, an uncommon mix. That first
morning, Tina hooked and promptly lost a trout that would have
been anyone's trophy, and hours later, as we sat down for a riverside
lunch, she fumbled with the food containers. She steadied herself,
then laughed, 'Man, I'm still shaking!'

A winged green stonefly, as large as a praying mantis, alighted
on her arm and we all studied it up close, and then Tina blew it
away gently as she would a butterfly. The stonefly sailed through
the air, and across the river.

'You can see why the fish here grow so big,' Christian said, and
in vain we rummaged through our fly boxes looking for a suitable
imitation. Size-wise, the Deer Hair Mouse was the closest we could
come up with.

THE TROUT BOHEMIA

With good friends on a good river, these were the perfect days, full of rare occasions, even if the cane rods, masterpieces of art that they were, stayed home, locked up in the Unimog.

It was again inspiring to see such harmony between two people. The same loving attention to detail that shone in Christian's rod-making and Tina's casting was clear in their togetherness, and how they expressed it towards each other. It was as if living together was a fragile art and only the daily observance of mastery and attentive care could turn it into a piece of work that was worth producing, and having. Living life as an art form, with the attention to every detail as important as the awareness of the big picture, here was a way for creating masterwork, whether a cane rod or a perfect cast, a story or a poem, a day on a trout river or a marriage. Life not imitating art but being it.

Back at the camp, we talked late into the nights, and not just about fishing.

'Our relationship is the most important to us,' Tina said. 'Everything else is secondary, whether we fish or hunt or laze about doing nothing.'

I thought that perhaps my own balance of priorities hadn't been in quite the right place. Well, it was too late now anyway. Maybe next time I'll do better.

I fell asleep to the river's lullaby, at peace with myself at last.

The encounter with Tina and Christian had also set my mind on casting again. Over the course of the season past, through fishing with top exponents like PJ and Miles, by growing into my own new rods and now experiencing the cane, I had been becoming increasingly unhappy with my casting, realising again just how much more there was to it than simply waving a stick back and forth, flopping out loops of line.

Like any biomechanical skill — a golf swing, swimming stroke or a ski turn — fly-casting has its proper and optimal form and its real-life application and often, through laziness, lack of attention or unconscious habits, the two can drift apart, which was what happened to me. I thought all my casting needed was a simple tune-up; hell, I used to teach it at one point. But it turned out too many years had passed and by now, with each cast I was just practising my bad habits, reinforcing mistakes. There was nothing else for it but to take my casting completely apart and back into its fundamental elements, then fix each of these in turn, and reassemble it all together. After the initial settling and wearing-in period, you wouldn't believe what a difference this had made.

If you really want to hone your casting skills, in New Zealand there is a one best place to go: the doll house of a tackle shop in Athol on the upper Mataura. It was autumn, nearly the end of the season. The days were already short and frosty but painted with gold of poplar and willow leaves, and one such crisp morning I met the shop's proprietor, Stu Tripney, for a three-day casting boot camp.

If you still have doubts about the existence of an archetypal 'trout bohemian', meeting Stu would dispel them for you once and for all. It would also redefine your ideas of what it means to be passionate about something. He is dyslexic with figures, his accountant's worst nightmare, but his love for fly-fishing burns bright, true and steady. Although he often works sixteen or eighteen-hour days — guiding, teaching, developing his signature foam flies, running the physical shop and its web-based offshoot — you get a sense that no matter what lucrative career opportunities would come his way, or if suddenly a fat inheritance cheque or a lottery win arrived in his mailbox, he would not change what he is doing now. And how many of us could claim just that?

At heart, Stu is still a Glasgow punk-rocker, with tats and studs, and the choice of wardrobe colours and music that go with it. He is perhaps best known for his innovative flies — realistic, slim and robust, and well thought out. Like his Pogo Nymph: a foam-body mayfly larvae imitation which, when held down by a heavier fly, bounces merrily near the bottom, looking and behaving just like the real thing.

But Stu is also the country's most qualified fly-casting instructor. Behind his tackle shop there is a grassy casting area with brightly coloured hula-hoops set up on stands to challenge the size of your casting loops. Tight loops are all the rage these days, unless you're using bamboo, but in 'casting according to Stu', the secrets of expertise are in understanding the mechanics of a good cast and then having the ability to adapt it to your requirements. Once you do that, you can cast any loops you want at any plane — vertical, sideways or off-shoulder — and that is imminently applicable in fishing.

'People often come to me psyched up for big trout and action-packed fishing,' he told me. 'I look at their casting and say: "Well, I can take your money, drag you around the river all day and show you the big fish but, casting like that, you haven't gotta show of catching them."'

This can be humbling for the clients and not the best self-marketing strategy for a guide but it keeps things honest, and it shows the clients up for who they are, whether true fly-fishers, albeit beginners, or just shoppers for trophy experiences, interested only in results and not the art itself.

'It's common for guys to buy these expensive rods believing that this'll fix their casting,' he said. 'I say to them: "If you spent the same money on yourself, on learning the skills, you'll cast better with a broomstick than you can now with this Ferrari of a fly rod."'

I had the Ferraris already, and no desire to go back to the broomstick.

'So how about it Stu?' I said. And so we began.

He asked me to cast short, medium and long lines, and as I did he walked around, taking in my performance from every angle. After a while I began to wonder: was it a frown on his face or was he just squinting into the low autumn sun? I thought I could cast reasonably well. Most people I fished with told me that too. Clearly, though, Stu did not share that opinion.

First, he corrected my grip. For short and medium casts the rod should be held like a hammer, with a slight kink in the thumb. For distance casting a key-grip was more efficient, holding the rod handle the way you would a key when you turn it in a door lock. The length of a casting stroke — how much the rod moved back and forth — had to be matched to the amount of line out in the air.

'Most anglers I see have the same casting stroke regardless of the distance they are trying to reach,' Stu said. 'That's why their cast is usually quite good at one particular distance, when the length of the line accidentally matches their rod action, but it falls apart at both ends, when they go short or beyond their usual length.'

Another common mistake was that the rod was never properly loaded, that no matter with how much vehemence it was being waved back and forth, it stayed more or less straight.

'It's like having that Ferrari and only driving it in the first gear,' Stu said, and it was obvious he had seen many of those.

Whatever your hand did the rod tip would do as well, and so it was imperative for the hand to travel in a straight line. This was called tracking.

'Best way to get that is to imagine you're painting a low ceiling with a brush or, even better, with a roller,' Stu explained. 'Nice and smooth, back and forth. Short strokes, long strokes, practise both as the action is the same, only the length changes. As you get better at that, you may start adding the wrist snap at the each end.'

This power snap of the wrist, a smooth acceleration to a crisp stop, is the most important ingredient of all. This is what gives the line its tight loop and the arrow-head aerodynamic profile which cuts through the air, and the wind, and which is much more efficient than a wide and slow 'elephant ear' loop that can get blown around and lacks accuracy.

The power snap is not a natural movement and so it needs to be practised diligently until it becomes an unvarying habit. A good training tool for that is Tim Rajeff's micro-practice rod. It looks like a kids' toy but is in fact a precise teaching aid, and the bright-coloured macramé yarn which acts as the fly line is so finely balanced it 'anchors' on the carpet like the line on the water so you can use it for roll and spey casts as well. Only when the power snap is firmly ingrained into your muscle memory can you start thinking about hauling, double-hauling and all the other fancy stuff.

I had two full days of this close analysis of my casting. My power snap was too fluffy, Stu had diagnosed, and so I practised it obsessively in every spare moment, while walking the dog along the river during our lunch break, and again in the evening when, sprawled out on big leather couches, we drank dark beer and watched hours of fish porn from Stu's extensive library. At times it felt I lost it altogether, that everything I did was wrong, and how on earth did I ever manage to catch fish casting like I had? But this was all good news because I knew from similar progressions in learning to ski that when it was all falling apart the most, the greatest improvements were being made.

On the third day we went fishing on a little Southland creek, full of brown trout and with not another angler in sight. We had discarded the teacher—student roles by now, and were but two friends on a river, drinking in the last of the season. Only then I realised that, living his dream lifestyle as he was, Stu had actually extremely little time to fish for himself. This added to the rarity of the moment. He was like a little kid again, just happy to be on the water.

He learnt to fish from his grandfather in Scotland where there was a fierce competitive spirit. 'Biggest fish I ever caught there was two pounds two ounces, and it won the entire comp and Grandpa and I were featured in the local paper. It was those two ounces that made all the difference.'

After the punk-rocker teenage years he cut loose from the gloom of Scottish suburbia and drove overland safari trucks in Africa. He guided people to see the mountain gorillas in Zaire and the elephants in the Okavango, ran a camp on the Zambezi, and caught tigerfish there. What he saw in his travels had redefined his values and priorities.

'We spent a lot of time among people who were really, really poor, by our standards anyways, Pygmies and other tribes,' he told me as we walked the creek, looking for fish. 'They had nothing but they were happy. Kids would play with an empty Coke can for months, kicking it around until it wore out. When I was a kid, I wanted a bike. My parents bought me a bike but it wasn't the one I wanted so I threw a tantrum, ruined the whole birthday. Man, for years later I felt so small and stupid for doing that, couldn't apologise enough to my folks for what they had given me. Africa is the best university of life you can ever go to.'

He ended up settling in New Zealand because of the trout. 'Fishing here was so much harder than anything I knew,' he said. 'For the first couple of seasons, like everyone else, I struggled to catch anything.' He realised that really good casting was one of the key skills he was missing but there was then no one around to teach him.

'Until recently there was no tradition of casting well in New Zealand, of improving and refining what you know,' he said. 'In the pioneering mentality of this country it was a simple act: a friend showed you how it was done and from then on you knew it. Your results in fishing were then just a matter of luck.'

But he wanted skills, to really understand casting, to get to the bottom of it. In this quest he tried to hire guides who were active at that time, but they too proved remarkably evasive. They could take him fishing, they said, but casting? Naw. It was something you just did. Flick the rod down, put the fly to the fish. There wasn't any more to it than that. And, for them, it was true.

For a while Stu persevered on his own, then he saw his opportunity. Patti Madsen, John Kent's fishing partner, was in New Zealand and she was one of the first Federation of Fly Fishers (FFF) casting instructors here. (The FFF is a US-based international non-profit organisation which, among other things, has set globally recognised standards in fly-casting.) She was about to fly back to the United States but agreed to meet the young and eager Scotsman. Stu travelled to have her look at his casting, a twelve-hour-return drive for a one-hour lesson.

That meeting was a turning point and it led Stu on an adept's journey from one teacher to another. Mindful fly-casting became his daily practice until, in 2007, he became Australasia's first FFF Master Caster. With all that came the realisation that there really was no bottom to it, no end to nuances and finesse, so that, like the Japanese tea ceremony, calligraphy or kung fu, fly-casting could be an art and a ritual in itself. Through it, you could strive for mastery, knowing all too well you would never reach it, but striving nonetheless.

So very Zen, you say, and you're right. Though, mind you, this was years before a book by a priest and a rabbi appeared on the angling scene. It was titled *Fly-fishing — The Sacred Art: Casting a Fly as a Spiritual Practice*.

Our autumn day on the creek was glorious in its golden perfection, but most of the fish were already in a spawning mood. They hovered over beds of fine gravel, guarding their real estate against intruders, jostling, swapping places, restless and on the move. At times the action in a pool would resemble snooker: one aggressive fish hitting a pod of several other trout and scattering them in all directions, arrowhead wakes erupting across glassy surface of the pool, ricocheting of its sides. Willow leaves, like wedges of gold, twirled down into the water and from a distance it was easy to mistake their touchdowns for rises.

Stu, for once not guiding or teaching but just fishing for himself, was soon lost in the joy of casting, of laying out perfect loops into most fishy places, forgoing the sight-fishing because in that mode he wouldn't get to cast anywhere near as much as he wanted to. I walked just ahead, leaving him to his pleasure, and here and there I found feeding fish, taking small grey mayflies that were alighting from the water. It wasn't a big hatch but a steady and consistent trickle, the kind you want and for which Southland's autumn is well known.

The feeding fish, the colour of burnished copper, were an easy target, usually a one-cast job but, inexplicably, each one I hooked turned and ran straight at me, so fast I had no hope of stripping the line tight. Each time it was a surprise and so I lost every single one of those fish, a long-range release right at my feet.

Stu laughed at my frustrations: 'Don't take it all so seriously,' he said. Again, not the kind of advice you'd expect from a guide.

On the next fish I was ready. It too ran straight back at me, but by this time I was also running, away from the creek. This was the only way to keep apace with these trout. I tripped and fell, got up with a kind of parachute roll, and kept running across the paddock, the rod held high, the line still tight. Stu was still in paroxysms of laughter when I finally netted the fish.

'Good thing you have enough backing on your reel. I thought you were gonna run all the way to Mossburn.' It was the nearest town, a good few miles away.

THE TROUT BOHEMIA

With the riddle solved, no more fish got away on us that day. My own casting felt shaky — there was too much new information yet to be integrated, too many changes to the old ways — but I didn't let it get in the way of living out this perfect day. I would have all winter to practise the Zen of casting, without the fish in sight to interrupt my focus.

Besides, Stu's light-hearted approach, his total and deliberate disregard for the pressure to perform, both in me and himself, was refreshing. So often in fishing the emphasis is so much on catching, on producing measurable results, that everything else, which is a much greater part of it all, gets lost or unnoticed. Stu is one of the few guides I'd ever met who focus not on the number of fish and their sizes but on the sheer undiluted pleasure of fishing no matter what the day brings, the delight of casting well, of being out on a river with passion that is alive and uncorrupted by the cynicism of business, untarnished by time and expectations.

'Do your fishing well and the catching will take care of itself,' he told me.

Hiring a guide like him was not so much a short cut to success but an invitation into the world of complexity and passion, a multi-layered reality that is fly-fishing.

On the way back to the truck I walked beside him, my right hand again, as if of its own volition, practising the power snap of the wrist.

'You've got it,' Stu said. 'You've got the bug of casting.'

Next thing, I thought, I'll be doing it in my sleep.

'These two guys from Turangi came into the shop once, both nearly at the end of their tether,' Stu said. 'They go: "Mate, we own a house on the Tongariro. We have a fish smoker in the backyard, we live on fish back home, and here we can't touch a thing." I says to them: "Brothers, I feel your pain. Years ago, it happened to me too. Come, let me offer you the cure to your problems."'

The two old trout dogs both had #8 wallopers of rods and casting strokes of backwoods axemen.

'It only took half a day to fix their casting and they couldn't believe how quickly they progressed to catching the difficult Mataura fish once they got their technique sorted. They thought I was a magician or something.'

Well, if he is then the rod is his magic wand.

Next time you think you need a better rod, consider a casting lesson first. With a bit of proper tuition the magic you seek is not that hard to conjure.

THE TROUT BOHEMIA

There were only two more days left of the river season in
Southland and, on my way back home, I revisited my River X, to
look for the last of the autumn hatches, to say my thanksgivings
and farewells before the valley would once more hibernate in fogs,
frosts and snow until another spring. Barry was there again, parked
in his one-man van in the public rest area under the willows, next
to a rickety wooden table. The tabletop was overflowing with his
food and cooking gear but he had cleared a strip of space along one
edge and on it he was repairing the tip section of his fly rod which,
it transpired, he had just broken on a fish.

By some uncanny coincidence, he was here parked in the same
place every time I visited this season — after the opening, then
again before Christmas, and now just before the end — and this
had created the illusion that he'd been here all this time.

The rod repair wasn't going well, the result about as nimble
as an arm in plaster, and after a while he gave up. The rod had
a lifetime warranty; it was easier to just get a replacement tip. I
offered him the use of one of my spares, but he promptly and
politely declined.

'Naw, I've caught plenty of fish,' he said. 'For this last day or
two I'm just happy to watch them. It's always such a buzz to see
them, isn't it? If you're fortunate enough you can . . .'

I suggested a drink and we took them down to the river and sat
on the high bank with our feet dangling over the water, watching a
few delicate emerger rises open and dissipate downstream of us.

'Best river in the world, isn't it?' Barry said, sipping his drink.

'Shush!' I cautioned. 'Someone might overhear us.'

He was a fishing guide for many years, Barry told me, catering
mainly for the Japanese clientele, back in the days when Japan's
economy was alive and well.

'Great clients, the Japanese,' he said. 'Always polite, quiet,
almost reverent of rivers and trout. Happy with whatever the day
brings, like all fishermen should be.' They were usually highly
skilled and superbly equipped, he went on, but had absolutely no
backcountry experience because, as one of them put it: 'in Japan
more fisherman than fish!'

Barry's face was oddly misshapen as if stitched from pieces
which, though seamless, did not quite fit together. I studied his
profile, and he caught me staring, and he said:

'Healed up well, didn't I?'

'What from?' I asked.

He was working in a motorboat yard, he said, selling and servicing all kinds of lake fishing craft. One day, he was replacing a big lead-acid battery, taking the fresh one off the charger, plugging the used one into the mains for a top up. It was a busy day, he got distracted, and when he brought the old battery for charging, he did not realise the charger was still on.

As he touched the crocodile clips to the terminals, bent over the battery which was on the ground, the battery exploded. The shrapnel of shattered plastic hit his face, followed by a spray of sulphuric acid.

'I had bits of plastic blown up my nose, right into the nasal cavity,' he said. 'Never knew pain like it.'

But worst of all was the acid in the eyes. When, after several operations, the docs took off the dressings and the bandages he could not see a thing. His visual world had gone blank and, in the shock of it all, the only thing he could think of was that he would never stalk and spot trout again, never gaze through the moving water to find their lithe and wondrous shapes underneath it.

It was grim to the extreme, he said. He fell into a bottomless depression. Life lost its meaning and purpose and he did not care for it any more. It was as if his entire world had disappeared, and he was left suspended in what seemed like a void but was in fact cluttered with a multitude of things he forever bumped into and tripped over. He stayed in bed for weeks, fearful to move, and in this private void his soul howled in agony.

The nurses would come and sponge and medicate his eyes, and massage his forehead and face, but every time he tried to open his eyelids he would get a head-splitting ache, a sensation that his brain was about to spill out through the eye sockets. Invariably, he would retreat into the void. At least there was no physical pain in there.

He did not know how much time was passing, days and weeks blurred into one another, but the pain was lessening. When he tried to use them, the eyelids would feel like they weren't his, barely responding to his will. But then something else happened. One day, the greyness of the void suddenly swirled and, in it, he was sure, he briefly 'saw' a hint of colour.

On impulse, still lying in his bed, Barry began exercising his eyes, first the eyelids, then the eyeballs as well. Open, shut, ten times. Rest, and repeat. Up, down, side to side, round one way, then the other. Hundreds of times, day after day.

When the eyes grew tired he would cup them with his palms and the resulting blackness was soothing and restful. Within it and over time, he perceived more blobs of colour which soon began to break up, colliding and exploding into rainbow fireworks, so bright they were almost painful. But he was excited now, on a mission to pull through. He knew he was getting better when, with the eyelids shut, his eyes started responding to sunlight, though at first no more than just reacting to the changes in its intensity.

This too he worked, letting the sun brighten the inner greyness, then resting the eyes in the darkness of his cupped palms, again and again.

After the colours came the shapes, fuzzy and indistinct at first, but a sure sign of progress. Barry redoubled his efforts, exercising his eyes for hours on end. It took months for the grey void to slowly disperse, for the world to acquire its forms again, its edges, then its details.

'I'll never forget the day I was back on the river and saw trout again,' he said. 'I know it may sound silly but the dream of that moment was what kept me going through all those months.'

I refilled our drinks and saw that Barry's hand was trembling.

'You don't realise what you have until you lose it,' he said. 'But if you're lucky enough to regain it, you'll never again take it for granted.'

He nodded towards the river.

'Look, there's a good fish coming across, it's now level with that big brown rock.'

I looked but could not see it. Then, ah, there it was, an indistinct yet so familiar shape ghosting over the golden pebbles, a sight that always brings joy to the heart.

'There is another one, three metres up from it,' I said and promptly took a swig from my cup, hoping the gin would soften the knot I felt in my throat.

Barry's eyes travelled up the line of current and he smiled.

'Yep, I see it, mate. I see it.'

And so for a long while we sat on the bank, watching the last of the season flow by, spotting trout, utterly content not to fish them.

Before I left, Barry showed me a picture of himself with a 17-lb rainbow he caught years ago in a river flowing into Lake Wakatipu. The fish was so large and heavy it was sagging in his arms, overflowing his grip. He carried the photo of it in his wallet, in a window of clear plastic usually reserved for the picture of a loved one.

THE TROUT BOHEMIA

chapter 15

'Good judgement comes from experience, and
experience comes from a lot of bad judgements.'

WILL ROGERS

One aspect of fly-fishing for trout I treasure above all else is the seasonal variety of our pursuit. The end-of-winter still water and the early-season nymphing on rivers where trout had lost the memory of anglers, the season's first mayflies, the arrival of green beetles with their metallic shine and antler-like antennae, the explosion of insect life in early summer. The fat bumbling cicadas and the trout that forsake reason and all sense to gorge on them, the willow-grub days when you can hear the fish slurping insects but you cannot see them in among branches trailing in the current, and later the much-anticipated spinner falls, when swirls of mayflies seem to be snowing out of clear autumn sky. And there are the surprises, of course, though more about one of them in a moment.

This is the trout calendar which I delight to live by. Within it — except for June, when the days are short and cold and often oppressed by the inversion layer of low grey clouds — there is always a time and place to go fishing somewhere good, even in the heart of winter. In fact, this winter fishing, when most anglers put away their gear and count down days towards the new season, has always held peculiar attraction for me, perhaps because some of my formative years as angler centred around Lake Taupo and its river mouths.

After the stealth and mileages which the season's sight-fishing demands, river time in winter is relaxing and sedentary, and far more social because all you need is a good spot and just enough room to cast, and so other anglers are no longer intruders on your river. I used to regularly travel to Taupo for a fix of winter fishing, a one-way drive of two and a half days in my trout camper. But as the peak of Taupo spawning runs became more and more unpredictable I looked for alternatives and found them, right at home, at the mouths of rivers which empty into the southern lakes. I got to know the river mouths of Lake Wanaka pretty well, with the runs peaking around mid-August when the snow lies low on the mountains and you often have to fish in neoprene gloves. But this time I ventured further afield, to explore the river drop-offs around Lake Wakatipu, and this is how I found myself fishing in Paradise.

For this particular jaunt I invited my new river companion Brendan, and his wife Rana, who travel in their own trout-mobile, a small 4x4 with a nifty and manoeuvrable caravan. Brendan is a Southland man, especially apt at small dry fly, and he was keen to learn winter fishing to which I professed a level of expertise. I had all the gear and he made himself a stripping basket, and we met in Glenorchy, an hour's drive west of Queenstown. I promised them a good time and surprises. If I had only known . . .

As fishing marriages go, these two are a success story, mainly

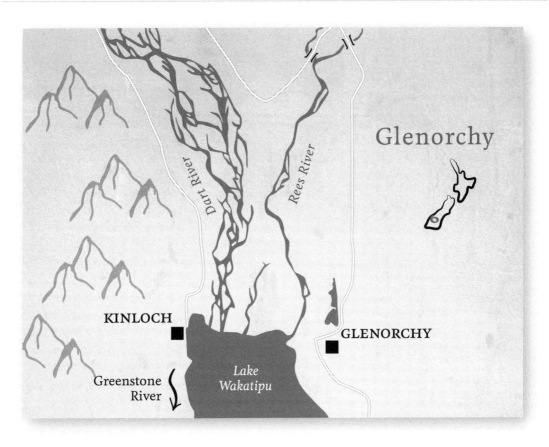

because Brendan only encourages and never insists, and he is quick
to praise to high heavens any fish his wife catches, often over the
trophy browns that mistake his fly for a natural. He worked for a
humanitarian agency out of Malta, survived dysentery in Ghana,
and his travels through tough places had inspired a calm and
pragmatism which permeate into his life and fishing, both of which
are inextricably intertwined. He would make a good guide, I often
thought, because he derives as much pleasure from seeing others
catching fish as from doing it himself. And this was exactly what
happened at our first stopover.

We began at the mouth of the Rees River which is near the
domain at Glenorchy's centre and I was like a hound out the gate,
wading across to the prime spot at the inside eddy, eager to demo
for Brendan just how things were done. At any river mouth an
eddy on one side of the current entering the lake is often more
pronounced than on the other, and this is indicated by flotsam
and bubble lines pooling around within it. You can reasonably
assume that trout food would be doing the same thing at the lake's

bottom just beyond the drop-off and that fish would treat such a place as a buffet and a prime beat to patrol.

In position, I was just stripping my shooting-head line off the reel, essing it out with the rod tip and against the current, when the line suddenly acquired a life of its own, straightening out into the deep water with such speed and purpose the backing had cut my fingers and drew blood. Fish! A good one, too!

By the time Brendan caught up I had the magnificent rainbow on the reel and in control, and I let him hear the zizz it was making peeling line off the spool, despite the drag being set on max.

'First cast! That's impressive,' Brendan nodded, and I could see he was already a convert to this winter fishing. It was impressive. We did not touch another fish for the rest of the afternoon.

Beyond Glenorchy, along the narrow gravel roads that branch out into the mountains, there are places with names like Paradise and Arcadia, which gives you an idea of the impact the beauty of this land had made on its pioneers. It would be harder to find more spectacular country, with the wide-open valleys fringed by forest, the shark-tooth Humboldt and Richardson Mountains forming the horizon, and iconic trout rivers like Greenstone, Rees and Dart entering the lake all within an easy drive.

You can ponder this from a purely aesthetic point of view until a practical realisation hits you: Wakatipu is a huge lake and full of fish. Just remember Barry's 17-lb monster. In winter, most of these fish are in spawning mode, and on the move. With the exceptions of those heading up the relatively smaller Lochy and Von, all of those fish have to spawn up one of the three said rivers and the mouths of these are like gateways through which all trout have to pass. All you have to do is to be there at the right time. Bit of a lottery? You bet.

I wondered about our timing as we drove around the head of the lake, set up a camp at the wooded beach of Kinloch and waded out into the delta of the Dart River. The Dart has several channels and each one ends in a textbook drop-off. Perfect water levels, well-defined eddies, no other fishermen. And no fish. We hooked one here and there, but it certainly wasn't the bonanza I had anticipated. To make things worse, a storm brewed up over the mountains and made the place look like Mordor. It rained, and then it snowed and, with each river having a huge mountain catchment, this made for dismal prospects. We started the next day with a long leisurely breakfast and talked about dry fly. Out of the caravan's window we could see the Dart running thick and grey like wet concrete.

When the storm cleared, the world appeared dazzling, freshened by new snow but largely unfishable, perhaps for a few days. In a last-hope attempt to rescue the trip I suggested we go exploring the mouth of the Greenstone. Unlike the braids of the Dart, all silt and shifting quicksands, the Greenstone's riverbed is cobbled and stable, the drop-off descending into the lake like a staircase. Even after heavy rain the river was running with only a hint of colour but clear enough to spot a couple of rainbows patrolling the edge of the deep. I cast a booby into the river, where it was still shallow, and let the current swing it over the drop-off, and I saw one of the fish accelerate towards it. The take was ferocious, but this time I was ready and let the backing run through my fingers, without cuts or tangles, with just enough pressure to allow a modicum of control.

I led the fish away from the action zone of the drop-off and into the slack water of the lake.

'Brendan, c'mon, there is another fish there,' I yelled. 'Get in there and catch it!'

But Brendan was gone. I looked around, widening my visual search, until I picked his figure along the beach maybe half a mile away. Out from him in the lake there was a sudden flash of silver as if someone had thrown a rock into the water and shattered its metallic sheen. A fish? In still water?

As I walked towards him I could not believe my eyes. The western shore of Wakatipu, on both sides of the Greenstone mouth, is sheltered by the Humboldt Mountains, a sharp wall of imposing crags, and so the waters here are still, even if there are whitecaps further out. In this glass-out, well within casting range, trout were dimpling the surface, rising to midges. In the middle of winter!

Did I mention that, in his journey as a fly-fisherman, Brendan was going through the midging phase? To him, every rise was a potential midge rise and to cover himself for the foreseeable and the unexpected he had tied an impressive array of innovative midge patterns. He never bothered to name any of them and just the previous night we entertained ourselves coming up with epithets and aliases for his creations. The all-time winner was the 'Crippled Spent Midge Emerger', the kind that requires a magnifying glass to see, let alone to thread on to the tippet.

Now, while loaded like a Mexican bandito with bandoliers of Stu Tripney's boobies, I was sulking that we did not quite hit the peak of the runs, Brendan was picking off one fish after another, with long precise casts and those inimitable midge patterns. He looked truly like an angler who had found his own paradise, a midge aficionado fishing to an untold number of midging trout, in the dead of winter and straight after a snow storm.

I tiptoed back not wanting to attract his attention and break the spell of the moment, taking the ability to derive pleasure from watching a friend catch fish to a whole new level. No choice really. Sure, there were enough rising fish to keep a platoon of anglers busy and content, and Brendan would certainly share his midge flies with me. But, in my single-minded focus on winter fishing, deep and heavy, I did not even have a floating line with me, an error I swear I shall never make again.

If you fancy winter fishing in Paradise, or at least near it, the most agreeable time is August and September, after the frigid inversion layer of early winter has burnt off. You'll still need neoprene waders because you would not last half an hour in your Gore-Texes and, as there is next to no walking involved, you cannot warm up that way. For drop-off fishing, a heavy sinking line, or better still a shooting-head, is required and the best and only flies are boobies, Woolly Buggers and smelt imitations. Wade out to about a rod's length from the drop-off and cast from there. This puts the line precisely where it needs to be and may save you from ending in the cold drink should the lip of the drop-off suddenly erode under your feet. And, of course, now that you know my sad story, don't forget a box of midges and a floating line should action break out in still water.

All three river mouths are easily accessible by road and viable even as a day trip from Queenstown. You just follow the lakeside corniche west and into the mountains, then turn off near a sign which says 'Paradise. No Exit.'

For a fly-fishing adept this seems a one-way sort of trip.

All season past I fished with intensity and abandon which surprised even myself. In the rivers and lakes of the Trout Bohemia I again found the best trout fishing I had ever known, and adventures with friends old and new, kindred spirits fuelled by the same passion. By all accounts, I should have been happy and fulfilled, and I was. Until I came back home for winter and had to face the demons of failure that were waiting for me there, and the growing realisation that all the travelling, and throwing myself into one escapade after another, was but running away from what mattered, and hurt, the most. By now I knew all too well that no matter how much I 'fished, and skied, and hunted, and went on long safaris', unlike the proverbial prince, I would not live happily ever after. Not without Ella.

Looking back at the season and the people I had met during my travels, it was clear I had learned as much about fishing and the country as about the nature of relationships, especially the ones that worked. If I knew then what I knew now how different things could have been, I thought. But isn't it always the case?

Still, there was no turning back time, nor was there any sense in even considering it. You cannot step into the same river twice; wise man Heraclitus had told us in his doctrine that 'change is the only constant'. Moving on with the flow of time, I thought that the least I could do was to put things to rest with Ella, try to remain friends after all the mayhem. I suggested we meet at the bench along the trail by our home river — we lived on the opposite banks — and to my surprise she agreed.

It was a cold evening, full moon glittering off the river, and we wore our down jackets, and almost like strangers sat on the two ends of the bench, and whether it was a bridge or a gulf between us I could not be sure. You cannot step into the same river twice; it is not the same river, and you are not the same person.

We talked for a long time, about how it was to be together, and how it felt to be apart. How it was a common if insane nature of the human condition that we so often had to lose something before we could truly appreciate just what we had, whether it was eyesight, a river or a person. Unlike me, Ella did not run away from her demons. She had been through hell, but she faced each emotional storm as it hit, and came out of it stronger and more resolved, more at peace.

I was surprised by the depth of her feelings, and by her wisdom, and even more by the fact that our first reconciliatory talk turned into a date, followed by others, increasingly more easy and intimate. After that first meeting I nearly flew back home on the wings of new hope, powered by another morsel of Heraclean wisdom: 'Opposition brings concord. Out of discord comes the fairest harmony.' The guy knew his rivers. I was sure I could trust his sagacity.

And they lived happily ever after? No such delusions, but who's to say, it's a work in progress. It calls for an utmost vigilance of moods, thoughts and inner states, and the ability — should they go foul — to not let them spill over and contaminate the space between us. It's the vigilance of a hunter, a fisherman stalking the river bank, all senses relaxed but alert, and that in itself is exhilarating with plenty of opportunities for the astronaut's prayer. For now, I'm shopping for those tango shoes. One day I may even bring out that bottle of Moët. Meanwhile, the learning never stops.

A while ago, sponsored by a cultural exchange of sorts, a group of Tibetan monks toured New Zealand. In a few selected towns, and Wanaka where I live happened to be one of them, the monks stayed for around two weeks, constructing a unique piece of art, a Buddhist mandala.

If you haven't seen one before, a mandala is a symbolic representation of the cosmos, a geometric model of the universe as seen from a human perspective, with all its beauty and the complexity of a puzzle. Most commonly, mandalas are circular, sometimes a circle within a square, and some are painted, but ours was made entirely of multicoloured sand. Its design was more elaborate than circuit boards of a mainframe computer.

The monks, with their copper pates, stubble haircuts and flowing plum robes, were a cheerful lot, boyish and happy, not immune to mischief. But they worked with a precision and focus that transcended the definitions of these words. They worked as if they were recreating the cosmos itself and in it, not a single grain of sand could be out of place.

First they had gone to the lake, found the right grade of sand, dug up the amount they needed, washed and dyed it with natural colours, then dried the sand in the sun so it poured like fine sugar. The workspace was set for them in the town hall where on a raised pedestal the monks placed a wooden board, the canvas for their painting. On to that board they poured their lines of coloured sand with funnel-like tools, over time forming a three-dimensional maze-like landscape of perfect mountains and valleys, each line a pyramidal ridge, a perfect sand dune no more than an inch high.

The work was highly ritualised, unrushed and deliberate, a prayer almost, not unlike I thought the way Ralph went about his fishing. It took the half-a-dozen monks two weeks to complete the mandala and all along you could come at any time to see their progress, though I assure you, seeing their single-minded intent, you would not dare to interrupt them with idle chatter.

The finished mandala was a good three metres across, a piece of work — like the universe itself — of bewildering complexity. After it was completed, there was a closing ceremony at the town hall and the place was so packed with people you could not move if your life had depended on it.

The atmosphere was charged, like the stillness before a thunderstorm. For a long while the monks gathered around the mandala were murmuring Tibetan litanies in low monotones, their voices as deep and resonant as didgeridoos. Then, with the same ritual attention to details, the same beatific smiles they wore during the work, the monks began to scrape the entire mandala off its base and into buckets, sweeping the board until it was clean and empty again.

There were gasps of disbelief in the audience as the spatula held by the lead monk bit into the mandala and scraped a path of destruction through the miniature landscape. Women wept openly and men in the audience showed severe symptoms of a jaw lock and cramped throats. It wasn't far from someone losing their cool and leaping on to the centre stage to stop this apparent desecration. Surely, a thing of such beauty should be preserved, mounted and displayed for all to see, now and for as long as it would last.

Alas, not keeping the mandala, not framing or mounting, not even photographing it, was precisely the lesson the good-hearted monks came to impart on their Western brethren. The joy was in the doing, and being your best while you did what you did. It was not in achieving or keeping the achievements, or worrying that something bad might happen to them, and, God forbid, getting them insured.

Thus the release was a natural conclusion to the circle of passion, pursuit and completion. It left the artists free and unencumbered, ready to continue on their quest. And so the monks took their buckets with sand, all that was now left of the mandala, and carried them to the lake from whence the sand came. They tipped up the buckets the way you may upturn your landing net and watched the content disappear in the water, blend in with its bottom. Then, with those same beatific happy smiles, they moved on.

And you thought catch and release was a fly-fishing concept.

Epilogue

'When we walk a river and don't see fish, we
leave the water undisturbed.'

CYRIL DARBEAUD

The new season has started and I am again answering the summons
of the trout waters. Like the last one, this spring too had been
volatile to the extreme, the country again an oceanic rock buffeted
by storms from every side. There had been more snow this spring
than during most of winter and, as I write this, my limbs still ache
from skiing the best powder snow we had this year, in the middle
of October.

Between the tempests, it had not been easy to find windows of
clarity, with conditions amenable to sight-fishing, but one day
I managed to explore with Brendan his favourite small creek in
Southland. During another clearing, with a coterie of local guides
searching for stormproof and flood-resistant waters — places to
go when all rivers are blown out — we found and fished the best
still-water flats I'd ever seen. Thus both days had been trophies to
keep and to relive in our memories even as we patiently wait for the
weather to stabilise, and for the season proper to begin.

Another highlight has been a postcard from Henry Spencer.
He was alive and well, never better, in fact. He had spent the past
season on a 'sabbatical' in Patagonia but was coming back later in
the year to fish in New Zealand again. It was easier to fish here, he
said. There was more variety and less distances and hard travelling.

There are so many waters to explore in our Trout Bohemia,
both new and old. Trout rivers are like good stories, revealing
themselves page by page, one twist or turn at a time. Interpreted
by an angler, they come alive with anticipation, surprises and
suspense. Unlike a story or a book, you can read a river many times
and — here's the wondrous part — every time it is different though
equally engaging. There are lifetimes of fly-fishing to be lived here
and never the same river twice.

I wish I could leave you with some utopian chocolate-box

image of our Trout Bohemia, and I'm sure the promoters of mass tourism would love that. The dirty if much denied truth, however, is that the best trout waters in the world are under an unprecedented threat from industrial rapacity and degradation, and no amount of 'Clean and Green' and '100% Pure' newspeak can cover it up any more.

As the global economic crisis spirals down ever deeper and the corporatism grows increasingly shameless, all stops are being pulled out to aid the so-called 'recovery'. In New Zealand, industrialised dairy farms have become the holy cow of the economy, and bogus corporate science has proven beyond all doubt that the rivers are best kept at their minimum flows, or even below, and that it's better like that for everyone, the farmers and the trout. What was previously unthinkable — mining in national parks, diluting the legal meaning of river conservation orders — is up for discussion now. There are even political arguments about who owns the water and how much this water should be worth. Perhaps the air will be next.

Some years ago I was in north-eastern Australia, on a magazine assignment about the Daintree rainforest, over a hundred million years old, a tiny and the last remaining sample of what all of Australia once looked like, before the continent dried up and turned into a desert. The scientists had installed a thirty-metre-high construction crane in the heart of that rainforest, and equipped it with a passenger gondola which gave them unlimited and non-invasive access to all layers of the forest canopy and its one-of-the-kind biodiversity.

The ride in the crane was interesting enough, but what really struck me then was that, in order for the rainforest and its surrounding ecosystem to be preserved, the conservationists in their despair were turning to the terminology of accountants.

'Tree-hugging and tearing of robes in front of bulldozers does little to stop the destruction of forests,' the lead scientist told me. 'We have to appeal to the decision-makers in their own language — the language of money. We must show them that a live forest is worth more than dead trees.'

To this end, one of their research projects was to quantify just how much the forests contributed to the quality of our lives. How much we would have to pay for their goods and services, were they to be provided by an outside contractor.

Daintree's ecological contribution was estimated at about two billion Australian dollars a year, but the global figures were astronomical. Valued conservatively, Nature's contribution was around US$33 trillion a year, twice the world's gross national product at the time. The inescapable question that occurred to me was: 'Impressive figures aside, just who else are we going to get to do the job?'

The same is now happening with our trout waters; they too are becoming a commodity valued in dollars — per litre, per tonne, per allocated rights. So I ask you: how low have we fallen to accept or even consider such discussions? Because, surely, talking about Nature's contribution in financial terms is like sending one's own mother out to whore and bean-count the proceeds, demanding not only that she provides for us but justifies her own keep as well.

Already in 1968, the inimitable Edward Abbey wrote that wilderness is not a luxury but a necessity for the human spirit, as vital to our lives as water and good bread. He went on to say that:

> A civilisation which destroys what little remains of the wild, the spare, the original, is cutting itself off from its origins, and betraying the principles of civilisation itself.

If only we had listened, not so much for the sake of the wilderness but for our own. Life on earth will continue, with or without us, so it is not so much a question of saving the planet but ourselves. Water — and trout water is almost always good water — is only part of this equation but one that we, as anglers, can do something about.

I believe that, as fly-fishermen and women, we know the rivers best. We are the first to see the signs of degradation, or improvement. If you consider the trout's habitat as an intricate web of rivers and lakes, streams and brooks — the bloodstream of the land — then isn't holding and feeling the fly line like measuring the pulse of the country, taking in its aquatic heartbeat?

As those who know the rivers, who see what is happening to them, we need to make a stand, together and alone, and simply say, 'Enough!' Water is life itself, its purity and abundance directly translating into the quality of our own existence. Who owns the water? How much is it worth? How arrogant to ask. How utterly insane.

For one, I am of good heart about all this. As the façades of delusion are crumbling, the truth about our place in the greater scheme of life shines through more and more, from behind the ruins of self-aggrandisement. Among other things, I draw solace and inspiration from the time I spent with the Kuku Yalanji people who have inhabited the Daintree for some 50,000 years and for whom the forest has been at once a library, a home, calendar, pantry and pharmacy — their entire world. They call it Marrdja, which roughly translates as the Boss.

Whether in the forests or rivers, the Boss will always have the final say.

When pursued at anything but a casual level, fly-fishing is a journey of self-improvement, an act of enquiry into the natural world. Sure the fish are the motivation and the reason, but only partly so. To insist that fly-fishing is all about catching fish is like saying the only reason for sex is procreation. In essence, yes, it is true, but how much we would be missing out on if the essence was all that there was.

Along the way on the fly-fishing path you may undergo a refinement — of gear, skills, approach and attitudes — from crude to ever more pure. As an evolution, this process has its own momentum, natural velocity and direction. Like any other evolution, too, it is a one-way trip. Once you take a step and move forwards, there is rarely a way of going back. Not that you can't, but you probably wouldn't want to.

I remember years ago teasing my fly-fishing friend Ian Cole about his obsessive insistence on sight-fishing. I was, I now see, like a child badgering the parent about matters it was yet to understand. 'Why do you need to see the fish first?' I asked him. 'You'll see eventually, at the latest when it's in the net.'

Nowadays, I sometimes feel a twinge of nostalgia for when I could simply go to a river, put on a dry fly as an indicator and a nymph to do most of the fishing, and cast for hours on end, in a happy state of blissful innocence and perpetual hope. I used to catch a lot more fish back then and the fishing had a certain baseline level of tranquillity and contentment, uncomplicated by hows and whys, and why nots. Such fishing was largely a matter of luck, although, if you put in the hours and the effort, this luck would usually reward your commitment and perseverance.

I cannot fish like that any more. It seems mechanical and un-engaging. The mind begins to wander, away from the present moment and usually upstream. 'There could be a fish by that tree up there and the water is shallow enough to see it.' Next moment I'm already there, looking. Seeing the fish first has become the Holy Grail of it all, not necessarily to catch it but to see it: the miracle in the water, a trout holding in the current, feeding with sinuous grace, dimpling the surface with its nose or fins, a masterpiece of Nature that we have found, the way a treasure hunter finds a nugget or a gemstone.

Years ago, I spent an enlightening couple of weeks with people who look for gold with super-sensitive metal detectors. Their quest is strangely akin to fly-fishing. They too seek trophies and weigh them, though in ounces not in pounds. The range is also similar: a ten would be a trophy, a seventeen the catch of a lifetime.

Their rods are like crutches, with a micro-computer on one end and a foot the size of a dinner plate at the other, the sensor to scan the ground with. Like trout fishers, they prospect the rivers, they helicopter up remote valleys and stay up there for days. Like us too, they have among them a code of silence: no names, no places, no amounts, no sizes. Bragging is a giveaway attribute of a newbie.

One main difference is that they hunt by sound, perceiving their world through high-quality headphones, instead of polarising glasses we use. With time and experience, you can differentiate the sounds made by scrap metal and other junk. You can tell not just whether it is lead shot, but what size it is as well. A nail, for example, gives off a sound like a whining cat. The sound of gold, on the other hand, is unlike any other, clear as a gong. As unmistakable as a soft-edged and fluid shape of a trout camouflaged against the rocks, under the skin of flowing water.

The prospectors could most likely get more gold using portable sluice-boxes or vacuum-cleaner-type dredges like Cavie had built. But, then, they would not be hunting. They would miss out on the thrill of the quest when in each moment all is possible, and a lifetime trophy could be just ahead. And so, like us, they prefer to remain hunters. They'd rather walk for hours and days, listening out for nuggets the way we look for trout — intent, focused, forced into being in the moment by the fear of what they may miss otherwise.

This approach has other advantages. In gold hunting as in fly-fishing, at the end of a blank day you can simply say you didn't hear any nuggets, saw no fish. In fishing at least this lets you off the hook for not catching anything.

In my own fly-angling journey this total conversion to sight-fishing had been a big and important step. I'm not sure where this evolution is leading me, but it seems to know the way and so I'm following along willingly.

There are moments in this style of fishing when the entire world stands still, when the fly has just landed on the water and it starts drifting towards the fish, and you can see it all. Take note of these silences because they are most precious. They are, I believe, one of the reasons why we fish.

There may be many instances of anticipation and excitement during a day's fishing but only watching the fly approaching the fish you are fully 'there' in the moment. No half-arsed interest, no banter, no distractions or multi-tasking. This is the Zen of fly-fishing. Watching the fly converge on the fish you are in 'The Zone', that mythical mind-space from which artists create, top athletes perform. In that moment, all your problems are gone, all the worries, and even if you have ailments of any kind most likely you cannot feel them there and then. No wonder Henry D. Thoreau wrote: 'Many men fish their whole life not realising it is not the fish they are after.'

Though I've come to think of New Zealand in this way, the true Trout Bohemia is not a place, a country, area or time, a trend or a group of people. It is a state of mind, a way of being, an appreciation for the ways of Nature, an openness towards its mysteries, and you can access it wherever in the world you might happen to be. It's in cooking on a campfire, drinking from a spring, waking up before sunrise to walk a river and to be mesmerised by it, to gaze through the veil of its surface, looking for a miracle, and finding it, again and again.

It matters not if you fish every day of a season, or just a week or weekend here and there. It is the quality of the direct experience that is the key to this magic. It may be elusive at first, but when you touch it once, and let yourself be touched by it, you will know it, and seek it again, and you will then always answer the summons of a river because it will feel like coming home.

Go to the trout waters, my friend. There, in these turbulent times, you will find what you need most. You may cast your flies, like Ralph, each time asking questions of the universe. But in the end, though the questions are interesting and finding answers is certainly gratifying, the trout waters and the silences we find there are more like a venerable Zen teacher.

They not so much offer answers to anything but make us stop asking so many questions.

From reviews for *The Trout Diaries*

‘Rarely has a book received so much universal praise as Derek Grzelewski's
THE TROUT DIARIES.’
American Angler

‘It is the best fly-fishing book I have read this year.’
Jeffrey Prest, *Trout Fisherman*, UK

‘Beautifully written and illustrated account of four seasons of fly-fishing
for trout and salmon in New Zealand.’
Gray's Sporting Journal, USA

‘I can't remember reading a better fishing book.
THE TROUT DIARIES will surely become a classic.’
Rob Sloane, editor, *Flylife*, Australia

‘Grzelewski can write. He has perfected the art of moving quickly . . .
Go with him and it may make you view your own journey with eyes
shining bright. Read it.’
Carl Walrond (author of *Survive!*), *New Zealand Geographic*

‘[This is a]. . . book that is set to open the world of fly-fishing to a
wider audience, with its elegant prose and passionate descriptions of
our beautiful country.’
Graham Beattie, *Beattie's Book Blog*